Peggy Davison Jenkins has specialized in education for creativity and has had many years of experience working with pre-school children. She has designed and taught classes and conducted community workshops for teachers and parents in which puppetry played an important role. She currently lives in Bellevue, Washington with her husband and two children.

The Magic of Puppetry:
A Guide For Those Working With Young Children

Peggy Davison Jenkins

PRENTICE-HALL, INC. A SPECTRUM BOOK Englewood Cliffs, N.J. 07632

Library of Congress Cataloging in Publication Data

Jenkins, Peggy Davison.
  The magic of puppetry.

  (A Spectrum book)
  Bibliography: p.
  1. Puppets and puppet-plays in education.
I. Title.
PN1979.E4J4   791.5'3   79-21907
ISBN 0-13-545152-3
ISBN 0-13-545145-0 pbk.

*To my mother
and my children, Gina and Ric,
who in their special ways
made this book possible.*

Editorial/production supervision and
    interior design by Carol Smith
Illustrations by Don Martinetti
Page layout by Mary Greey
Manufacturing buyer: Cathie Lenard

© 1980 by Prentice-Hall, Inc.
Englewood Cliffs, New Jersey 07632

A SPECTRUM BOOK

Printed in the United States of America

10   9   8   7   6   5   4   3   2   1

PRENTICE-HALL INTERNATIONAL, INC., *London*
PRENTICE-HALL OF AUSTRALIA PTY., LIMITED, *Sydney*
PRENTICE-HALL OF CANADA, LTD., *Toronto*
PRENTICE-HALL OF INDIA PRIVATE, LIMITED, *New Delhi*
PRENTICE-HALL OF JAPAN, INC., *Tokyo*
PRENTICE-HALL OF SOUTHEAST ASIA PTE., LTD., *Singapore*
WHITEHALL BOOKS, LIMITED, *Wellington, New Zealand*

Contents

Foreword

I highly recommend *The Magic of Puppetry* to all who have anything to do with the young—and not just the very, very young. There are answers for every possible puppet question a teacher could ask—and many for the questions a beginner would not even think to ask.

While reading it for the first time, I kept saying, "Yes, yes! That's so true!" And most telling of all, "Why didn't I think of that?"

Many of Peggy D. Jenkins's suggestions remind me of things I always do and enjoy in puppeteering. These things, such as developing the puppet's character through play or just fooling around, are so very important. In preparing shows with grown-up puppeteers, I like to have one silly session where we go wild with the characters and do and say all the crazy things that have been suppressed during the serious, laborious rehearsals. Out of such sessions come many useful ideas in dialogue and manipulation.

Children are usually much less inhibited than adults. It's easier for them to let their imaginations run wild. Imagination, to me, is one of the most important things in life. How can an architect design a bungalow or a palace without first seeing the structure in his head? How can a composer write the melodies without first hearing them in her head? Imagination does not belong only to dreamers. Everyone's life is richer for having it. Anything that helps children expand their world should be encouraged.

Only someone very dedicated to both children and puppets could have written this book. It should be required reading for anyone starting a puppet project with children. Peggy Jenkins has thought of everything!

Tom Tichenor

Preface

The purpose of this book is to help those working with young children understand the value of puppetry for children and to show simple and effective ways to make and use puppets in furthering children's education and development.

The young children I am referring to are the three to nine age group, although most of the puppets and ideas presented here can be enjoyed clear into adulthood. The more complex puppets and information have been left out, because there are already adequate books that deal with them.

When I wrote *The Magic of Puppetry* in 1971, I felt there was a need for a book that emphasized instant puppets for the beginning puppeteer and ideas for getting started using puppets in a creative way. That need is stronger than ever and is the reason for writing this revised and expanded version. So many books neglect the use of the puppet once it is made except for offering a few plays. Sometimes these are original plays and, therefore, a creative experience for the writer, but seldom is doing someone else's play going to stimulate a child's creative imagination. More often, it's going to thwart it if too much emphasis is put on the "one right way." My hope is that the emphasis during all stages of puppetry be put on the creative process and not the finished product.

Those of us working with young children (teachers, parents, librarians, club directors, baby-sitters, and so on) sometimes get our means mixed up with our ends. We want to encourage such needed attributes in children as creative thinking, imagination, independence, spontaneity of expression, and constructive release of tension. We hear that puppetry and art and creative drama are great means to this end. But what happens? Too often the means become the end. We lose sight of our goal and put our emphasis on a finished product, be it artwork, play, or puppet. Instead of encouraging children's ideas, we tell them just what to do or make—with the result that their imaginations are stifled, their expression inhibited, and their tensions increased.

It is my hope that those who use this book will keep in mind the need for creative thinkers in today's world and will use puppetry as a means to help fill that need. Encouraging creativity involves drawing out children's talent, valuing their ideas, and providing a creative climate. The creative climate is one that offers psychological freedom and psychological safety. This kind of climate grows out of love—genuine love, which is unconditional acceptance. This kind of acceptance can exist only when we separate a person from his or her behavior. We are then free to love that individual completely and to approve or disapprove only of the behavior. We appreciate or dislike the child's acts, but the child's worth as a person is understood and not questioned. It is this kind of safe, accepting, nonjudgmental climate that builds sound self-esteem. There is no more important goal, I feel, for those working with children. Children's feelings about themselves affect their achievement in all areas of their lives.

Adults' feelings about themselves must also be considered in this area of puppetry. Often those working with children feel hesitant about getting into puppetry if they are not craftspeople or artistically inclined. Many gifts are used in puppetry, and it is the rare individual who has them all. The most important gift, in my mind, is the ability to draw out a child's creativity and build his or her self-esteem. If the creative process is important and not the finished product, what does it matter if the instructor cannot paint an artistic backdrop or is all thumbs at sewing and gluing? If instructors are truly separating themselves from their own behavior, then they cannot possibly feel inadequate for these shortcomings.

Since models usually inhibit rather than encourage creativity, there is no need for the instructor to do any more than motivate and guide the children. This is where his or her creativity is challenged. And as we use our creativity, it grows, just like a muscle that is exercised. We need to accept and encourage our own ideas just as we would a child's when we are trying to stimulate that youthful creativity. If we judge our creative sparks, they may withdraw like a child who is put down, but when we don't judge, more will come through. We can then grow in creativity along with the children we instruct.

Acknowledgments

I must share the credit for this book with the many people who have expanded my knowledge in the field of puppetry. They include all of the puppetry authors I have read, the puppeteers I've known and observed, the children and teachers I've taught and who have taught me. In one way or another, they all contributed to this book.

Special recognition goes to Professor Margaret S. Woods of Seattle Pacific University. It was her emphasis on education for creativity which inspired me to search for means to this end.

I am deeply indebted to Margaret Davison for her encouragement, editing, and support.

With all of the above, the book could have still remained unpublished if it had not had the good fortune to come to the attention of two people with vision and authority: editor Mary Kennan and puppeteer Tom Tichenor. I am especially grateful to both of them.

Welcome
to the
Magic World
of Puppetry!

There is magic in puppetry for children of all ages, seven to seventy. Wherever people let "the child within come out to play," puppets find eager acceptance because of the magical world puppets open up.

They are magic because through our thoughts and our actions, they can be anything we want them to be. The puppet's life comes from our heart as well as our hands. The heart is where magic begins.

Puppets have a long and interesting history in many parts of the world, where their magic was as important to the adult population as to the young people. That puppets have been around for centuries suggests the need they have fulfilled.

This magic was recognized by Goethe when he said, "This childish entertainment and activity produced in me such a capability to create and to act, and exercised and demanded such skill and technique, as perhaps could have occurred in no other way, in so short a time and confined a space." Also attesting to the special quality of puppets, George Bernard Shaw once wrote that the dramatic influence puppets had on him was greater than that of live actors.

Where imagination and invention are more important than material substance, there is bound to be magic. That is puppetry!

It is hoped that the ideas in this book will help you and the children in your life get a little closer to that magic within—to that uniqueness that is at the center of each of us—and that this will be brought forth and shared with the world.

1

A
Philosophy
of Puppetry

These statements are the foundation for achieving the values of puppetry described in the next pages.

- Puppetry is an art—a performing art. All children deserve to try out their skills in all the arts. This art form is so all-encompassing that a child actually gets to practice a great many arts through it.

- The emphasis in puppetry should be on the use of the puppet and not on the making of it. It should be introduced, not as a craft, but as a performing art.

- Puppets should be experienced first, so that the desire to make puppets will grow out of this experience. Thus adult and child usage should precede the making.

- In making puppets, it is best to keep in mind that the puppet is a means to an end, rather than an end in itself. It's an instrument.

- Making a puppet without knowing why it is being made or how it will be used is best avoided.

- Instant puppets, quick to make, are best for young children.

- The puppet's movements are important—as important as the words it says. Movement is the essence of the art.

- Puppetry should be <u>fun</u>. Learning can be fun through puppets.

2

The Values of Puppetry for Children

Puppets fascinate and involve children in a way that few other art forms can. It may be because they allow children to enter the world of fantasy so easily. In this magic world, children are free to create whatever is needed right then in their lives. Because puppets often reveal the inner world of the child, a great deal can be accomplished through puppetry.

Here, presented in random order, are some of the main values of puppetry for the young child:

PUPPETRY LEADS TO CREATIVE THINKING AND USE OF THE IMAGINATION Almost every stage or step of puppetry calls for the use of creative imagination, and it is this faculty that so needs to be developed in today's youngsters. Most of the education process tends to stamp out imagination, which is the source of answers to individual, community, and global problems. Imagination is also a significant enhancer of later learning, as studies at Wayne University have shown. Young children who had been involved in ''pretend'' play showed marked superiority four years later in concept learning and in inhibiting impulsive behavior. Puppetry allows the audiences, too, to use their imaginations, since they must fill in the nonexistent aspects of the setting, the puppets' features, and so forth.

PUPPETRY ALLOWS THE CHILD TO TEST LIFE SITUATIONS VI- CARIOUSLY Puppets enable the individual to experiment with ideas and desires that he or she has not yet faced in actual life. They provide the opportunity to indulge in fantasy in a healthy way and to practice short-term goals. For instance, a child who is apprehensive about attending a birthday party might rehearse the event with puppets.

PUPPETRY HELPS CHILDREN TO RECOGNIZE THEIR OWN BEHAVIOR—TO SEE THEMSELVES Awareness of self can prompt a change in be- havior. Through observing the unhappiness of the timid or the overly aggressive puppet, children may alter their methods of reaction.

PUPPETRY OFFERS THERAPEUTIC VALUE THROUGH DRAMATIC PLAY BY EXPOSING HIDDEN ANXIETIES, RELEASING TENSIONS, ETC. Puppets provide individuals under stress with an opportunity for ''projecting'' on inanimate objects. It is well to remember that unexpressed negative feelings can have a damaging effect on health—physical and mental. This is because ''thoughts held in mind, produce after their kind.'' Through puppetry, emotional stress can be released and dispelled in a harmless manner. It is a great safety valve.

PUPPETRY AIDS IN DIAGNOSTIC WORK DONE BY SPEECH THERAPISTS, PLAY THERAPISTS, PSYCHOLOGISTS, AND SOCIAL WORKERS For in- stance, one speech therapist has all the elementary children say key sentences to her puppet in order to identify those needing help. Through the use of puppets, children may reveal subcon- scious attitudes and indicate certain problem areas within their world. The wise leader finds time to talk about these and resolve any misconceptions on the part of the child.

PUPPETRY OFFERS THE CHILD AN AVENUE OF EXPRESSION WITHOUT FEAR OF NONACCEPTANCE This partially accounts for so much of the hitting done by puppets. Also, puppets don't have to sing on tune, or be able to pronounce all their words correctly, or re-

The Values of Puppetry for Children

member the punch line to a joke, or be a perfectionist in any way. A puppet spells security.

PUPPETRY TAKES PRESSURE OF BLAME OFF THE CHILD AFTER MISTAKES HAVE BEEN MADE Children really can and do disassociate themselves from their puppets' mistakes. After all, it is the puppet that is clumsy or stupid, not the person operating it.

PUPPETRY FREES YOUNGSTERS FROM SELF-CONSCIOUSNESS, THUS HELPING OVERCOME SHYNESS AND STUTTERING Usually, children will not stutter as long as they keep their eyes on the puppet who is talking for them. Shy children are usually more outgoing with a puppet in their hands. Children who won't sing or speak above a whisper will often perform beautifully through a puppet.

PUPPETRY ENCOURAGES DEVELOPMENT OF COMMUNICATION SKILLS The child is required to think out his or her words carefully so that his ideas will be understood by others. Children whose speech sounds are defective, distorted, or omitted will gain incentive to improve their speech so that the puppets will be understood by their classmates.

PUPPETRY DEVELOPS CRITICAL LISTENING SKILLS AND THE ABILITY TO THINK QUICKLY Children involved in skits are challenged to listen attentively in order to respond appropriately and rapidly.

PUPPETRY INCREASES ATTENTION SPAN Parents and teachers alike have been amazed at how much longer children listen when a puppet does the teaching.

PUPPETRY AIDS IN LEARNING The novelty of the educational device helps youngsters retain new information. This is true whether the teacher or the child is using the puppet. An old proverb says: "I hear, but I forget; I see, and I remember; I do, and I understand." That capsulizes why puppetry enhances any learning experience.

13

PUPPETRY PROVIDES OPPORTUNITY TO WORK COOPERATIVELY AND SHARE IDEAS WITH PEERS A puppet show is a tremendous means of encouraging teamwork in the classroom and elsewhere. This team-building aspect makes it a good activity for families, clubs, and other groups.

PUPPETRY OFFERS MUCH OPPORTUNITY FOR PROBLEM SOLVING Rather than dealing with theoretical problems, puppetry provides youngsters with much needed exercise in practical problem solving. If the challenges of puppet making, script creating, staging, and so on involve the children and not the adult, there will be an endless array of meaningful problems for them to cope with.

PUPPETRY CONTRIBUTES IN MANY WAYS TOWARD SOUND SELF-ESTEEM Sound self-esteem is feeling warm and loving toward oneself. It's unconditional self-acceptance. Many teachers are using puppets in planned situations to foster these good feelings about the self. Often, children can accept positive affirmations from a puppet that they can't from an adult. The puppet can treat the children as if they already are all that they are individually able to be. Belief in themselves is instilled.

PUPPETRY HELPS BUILD A POSITIVE SELF-IMAGE This refers to how we see ourselves and differs from the feeling or emotion of self-esteem. There are so many aspects to puppetry that usually a child will find some area to excel in—script writing, ''prop'' ideas, puppet design, expressive movement, use of voice, stage building, music ideas, and so forth. Students who do not do well in academic subjects frequently have their first success through puppetry. This has been enough to change their self-image so that other successes followed.

PUPPETRY GIVES THE CHILD A SKILL THAT CAN BE USED ALMOST EVERYWHERE TO SATISFY THE NEED FOR RECOGNITION AND FOR ENTERTAINING OTHERS Often at school, camp, or parties, children are asked to make a contribution to the entertainment. At family gatherings, children welcome a positive way to receive recognition. Familiarity with puppetry and instant puppets can provide just the right answer for some children. It is a resource they can use at the drop of a hat, wherever they may be.

PUPPETRY ACTS AS A VEHICLE FOR BUDDING ARTISTIC AND DRAMATIC TALENT It certainly can aid children in learning all phases of drama, and there is no end to the art media that can be employed in constructing puppets. These can expand with the development of the child.

PUPPETRY INTEGRATES SUCH INSTRUCTIONAL AREAS AS ART, LITERATURE, SPEECH, MUSIC, SOCIAL STUDIES, SCIENCE, ARITHMETIC, AND MANY OTHERS This integration compounds the educational value of the material studied and makes for more thorough learning.

PUPPETRY DEVELOPS MANUAL DEXTERITY AND MANIPULATIVE SKILLS Physical therapists often use hand or finger puppets to strengthen the muscles of patients.

PUPPETRY HELPS CREATE NEW INTERESTS Arts and crafts, sewing, drama, music, construction, story telling, and singing are a few of the interests that could develop through exposure to puppetry.

PUPPETRY AIDS IN THE DEVELOPMENT OF ATTITUDES Puppets are a really superior tool for helping children form finer attitudes. Many teachers feel that positive attitudes can be more significant for a child's future than all the academic subjects combined. An example of puppetry in the attitudinal change area is a study kit including six puppets being used in classrooms to teach children sensitivity toward their handicapped peers.

PUPPETRY PROVIDES FUN This is an often neglected value in our culture.

It is hoped that this list, although incomplete, shows that every well-designed puppetry experience will achieve some of

15

these values. If most of the available time were spent on making the puppet, rather than using it, many of the foregoing values would not be attained.

3

What Is a Puppet?

A puppet is any sculptural or pictorial representation that is made to move by the efforts of an operator. It can represent anything—animals, people, inanimate objects, or abstract ideas.

Some call the puppet a "man-made actor." Others define it as an object without life that is treated as real. This means that almost any inanimate object can become a puppet if it's brought to life by a performer. It's the performer's imagination that is the catalyst. A spatula, hammer, twig, or detergent bottle, when used in a creative way, can become more a true puppet than an elaborate commercial puppet that remains immobile. To "live," a puppet must be given personality by a human operator.

4
Types of Puppets

Following are the seven types of puppets in common use and an eighth unusual type:

String Puppets
Rod Puppets
Stick Puppets
Shadow Puppets

Hand Puppets
Finger Puppets
People Puppets
Invisible Puppets

The above puppets are classified according to the method of control, but puppets can be classified in many ways. They can be classified by the country of origin, by whether they are worked from above or below, by whether they are flat or solid, or by whether the substance or only the shadow is seen.

Listed next are brief definitions and descriptions of these eight categories of puppets. There are, of course, hybrid puppets that combine the features of two or more types.

String Puppets

Also called marionettes, string puppets are controlled from above by wires or strings. They are fascinating but hard for children to make and to work. Puppeteer Tom Tichenor says marionettes are the problem puppets, where perseverance, patience, and practice are required—all three in large quantities. For these reasons, it is recommended that they not be made or used below the fifth grade. Even the simple two-string puppets are frustrating for the young child because of the constant twisting of strings.

The adult who wishes to use this type to entertain children can make a simple H of two thicknesses of fabric, put spools or weights of some type in the legs, attach a soft ball-shaped head and two strings, and then add the final features.

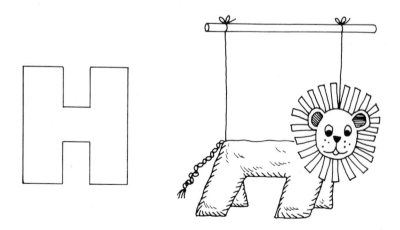

Probably the two-string puppet that's easiest to make is simply two strings attached to a balloon. (To glue on features, use rubber cement because plastic glue will pop the balloon, as will permanent felt pens.)

Rod Puppets

A rod puppet can be more complex than a string puppet or almost as simple as a stick puppet. Like hand puppets, they are usually held above the performer's head. There are many variations of rod puppets, but they usually have a long rod to swivel the head and a shorter rod or wire to move each hand. It is felt that they also are better for older rather than younger children because of difficulties in making and using them.

Stick Puppets

The simplest of all puppets, stick puppets are controlled by a single stick (any slim, rigid support) that goes up inside the puppet or is attached to the back of it. With this, the puppet is moved around the stage or turned from side to side. These have the advantage of being a good first puppet for preschoolers, as a stick can be attached to any little doll, toy animal, cutout figure, fruit, or vegetable, and they are most easy to operate. Chapter 9 on instant puppets has many suggestions for stick puppets.

Shadow Puppets

Shadow puppets are figures that appear on a screen because of the arrangement of light behind them. They are usually flat, cutout figures made of cardboard or other heavy material. Usually they are attached to a stick like a stick puppet or dangled from a stick by means of a thread or moved by a wire attached at right angles to the puppet. Hand shadows also make a type of shadow puppet.

There are two general approaches to shadow puppets. They can be used in front of a light screen or behind a shadow screen. In the first instance, the light of some kind of projector or lamp is used, and their shadow is cast on a screen or white sheet. With the latter, the puppet is held against a translucent screen that is lighted from behind. Easy screens and quick shadow puppets are mentioned in Chapter 9.

Shadow puppets have the advantage of deep emotional appeal, and a single puppet can take on many sizes and shapes through a change in the position of the light or the puppets.

Hand Puppets

Hand puppets, frequently called glove or mitten puppets, are the most popular for young children. There are many types of hand puppets, but most can be classified into two general groups:

- those with moving mouths

- those with moving hands.

The first is any sort of hand covering—a handkerchief, a sock, a mitten, a paper bag—inside of which one's fingers open and shut, forming the mouth of the puppet.

The second kind of hand puppet is one that has a head and two hands and is operated by putting one or two fingers in the head and one in each hand. This kind of hand puppet can freely pick up objects and make hand motions, thus putting more realism into a performance. The other kind of hand puppet, however, has the advantage of being able to "talk." There are also two-hand puppets, where one hand works the puppet's mouth and the other works one of its hands. This puppet seems very real because with two hands in it, you can make it do almost anything.

Finger Puppets

The three general types of finger puppets are:

• Finger-Leg—those where two fingers (index and middle) serve as the puppet's legs.

• Finger-Cap—those that slip over an individual finger.

• Finger-Face—those where faces are drawn with felt pen on the finger itself. Usually, one can perform with quite a few puppets of this type at one time. They are great for finger plays.

The many advantages of finger puppets include the following:

• They're easy to manipulate, even by a toddler.

• Individual finger action is encouraged.

• They're inexpensive to make.

• One child alone can put on a performance with a whole cast.

• They're small enough to carry easily and use when traveling or visiting.

• They're good for a child sick in bed, because their use is not tiring.

• They maintain interest because they are easy and quick to construct.

• They can be made in spare moments, since materials are small and mobile.

• They take up little storage space.

• Their stage is small, inexpensive, and simple to make.

People Puppets

People puppets are also called bib puppets or humanettes because they are half person and half puppet. A bib puppet is actually a cardboard puppet without a head that is tied around the actor's neck like a bib. The easiest people puppet for young children is a large paper sack put over the head. Holes are cut out for the eyes, and facial features and decorations are added with paint or paper and paste. The bags can be turned up slightly above the shoulder or cut away on the sides. People puppets make a natural transition from puppetry to creative drama. Also, shy children generally feel more protected behind this kind of puppet than the others.

Invisible Puppets

Here is a puppet everyone can make, and the price is right. No materials are required. All that is needed is an active imagination. The invisible puppet, more than any other, demands the use of creative imagination by the observer as well as the puppeteer. The puppeteer has to make the observer see this imaginary puppet through what he or she says, and the observer is challenged to see and to feel.

The invisible puppet is the peak of the imaginative process because there isn't anything it can't do. It can appear and disappear at will, walk across the ceiling, master any game or stunt, and walk through walls—to name just a few of its possibilities.

The invisible puppet is labeled a puppet rather than an imaginary person to ensure that the child who tends to get reality and fantasy mixed up knows that it is fantasy.

These puppets help children disclose a lot of themselves, and they aid growth in the area of communication. They are always readily available and can even be used while driving the car or doing dishes.

A few ideas for getting started are presented in Chapter 9.

5

Dramatic Play
and
Creative Drama

When used by children, puppets are tools for either dramatic play or creative drama.

Puppetry as <u>dramatic play</u> refers to spontaneous dramatization where the child has the freedom to <u>express him- or herself spontaneously</u> through identification with the puppet. Role playing, singing, and acting out familiar stories may result, but they grow out of the needs and interests of the child at that particular moment.

Puppetry as <u>creative drama</u> simply refers to any type of creative dramatics where the child plays his or her role through the puppet.

Puppetry as Dramatic Play

Puppetry with young children (ages three to nine) is most effective and meaningful when it is used as an aspect of dramatic play rather than as creative drama. Sophisticated puppet presentations where the final product is emphasized tend to get in the way of individual needs and are inappropriate at this age.

The main requirement in encouraging the use of puppets for dramatic play is to have plenty of them available at all times and/or a "puppet stuff box" with materials for making instant puppets. A lot of applause and appreciation from you is also an essential ingredient.

Children are also more inclined to use puppets if they have first seen them in use. So use them yourself, and expose the children to the puppetry of others. Sing them a song, or tell a story or riddle with a puppet, and they will likely be doing the same thing next day.

When the enthusiasm for dramatic play subsides, consider the following ideas to revive a lagging interest:

- contribute a new puppet

- make a puppet together

- provide another type of staging

- obtain some props for puppets to use—hats, tools, baskets, mirrors, books, and so on

- attend a puppet performance

38

- make a simple stand with vertical dowels to display puppets invitingly

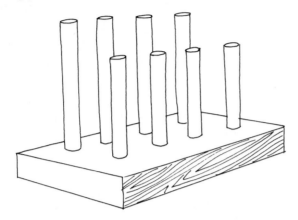

- provide a large mirror for puppeteers to view their manipulations.

Puppetry as Creative Drama

Simple situations, rather than stories, are best for beginning dramatics. Children can gain experience through such puppet activities as a tug-of-war, washing floors and windows, telling riddles, doing a song and dance act, or putting props onstage for an imaginary play. In fact, this last has been done as a complete play in itself.

One of the easiest ways for children to start using puppets is with riddles. One child with two puppets or two children can put on quite an act. The libraries are full of riddle books, and some puppeteers like the security of having memorized a few riddles and jokes. One boy used a series of "Knock, Knock, Who's There" riddles and worked up a skit complete with motions.

From such simple situations, the children may want to move on to acting out nursery rhymes, folktales, and Aesop's

39

fables. Some authorities feel this is an important experience before writing one's own play, because it gives the basic feeling for plot so often missing in original plays. My own preference is to encourage children to make up plays of their own, even though they're not dramatically perfect. There is a thrill and benefit in creating that cannot be realized when only interpreting the ideas of others.

Almost every puppetry book includes two or three plays. But how much more the children will get from the experience when they have created their own play or have at least made their own adaptation of a favorite story. One way to do this is to rewrite a fairy tale. They might poke fun at the characters, put them in a supermodern setting, make up a surprise ending, or combine the characters in one story with those in another.

In Howard's *Puppet and Pantomime Plays*, most of the plays suggested do not dictate to the children but encourage them to come up with ideas of their own. Even the few that are specific leave room for the children to use their own words. With most published plays, the author has already had most of the creative experience. Repeating someone else's words does not do much to develop a child's creative thinking ability.

Creating a Play

There are two approaches to creating a play—the planned and the unplanned. The latter is where the child is given puppets and lets them speak in an impromptu manner as suggested by the characters and situations. This "act-as-you-go" puppetry is very much like dramatic play but somewhat less spontaneous.

When planning a play, there are also two approaches. One is to make the puppets first (or use already made ones) and plan a play suggested by the puppets. The other approach is to plan a story and then make the puppets to suit it. Some feel that this method is easier and safer, because the story is likely to be less forced. There are advantages to both, depending upon what your goals are. Certainly the creative problem solving that would result from trying to build a story around a certain four puppets—say, a king, a girl, a wolf, and a frog—would be most

40

worthwhile and would give the child a starting place for his or her thinking. Other good ideas are to take a familiar "people" story and adapt it to animals, or to take an old favorite and put on an entirely new beginning or ending.

If older children wish to create an original puppet play, there are a number of things that need to be kept in mind:

- The play needs a plot, which consists of a conflict or apparently insoluble problem with an ingenious solution.

- Like any play, it should have an introduction, body, and conclusion. The problem is introduced, there are attempts to solve it, and a satisfying ending is reached. The play should end as soon as possible after the problem is solved.

- The story should have plenty of <u>action</u>. Puppets are not good for long, talky material.

- The script lines should not be memorized but improvised, in keeping with the structure.

- The puppets should keep in character (funny, worried, bossy) throughout the whole play.

- The unique ability of puppets to do things that are impossible for people should be remembered (fly, disappear, and the like).

- It is best to get the audience involved whenever possible. Having them help the characters adds to their enjoyment of the play. This is one of the strengths of puppetry—it gets <u>all</u> the children involved, not just the performers.

- Avoid lengthy plays. A good puppet story can be told in five or ten minutes.

It is important that the children learn through their own experience and without adult plans or preconceived notions of

41

what the play should be like. There is plenty of time later in life for assimilating adult ideas, but a lot of valuable imagination can be lost if it is not developed in childhood.

The Use of
Puppets
in the Home,
School, and
Elsewhere

The use of puppets is deliberately presented before the making of puppets because it is felt that familiarity with puppets will stimulate a real desire for creating them. There is usually no real feeling for making puppets if children have not had some exposure to them.

Some of the places where puppets are creatively used by both child and adult include the home, classroom, Sunday school, library, hospital, Scout or Campfire meeting, camp, counselor's office, psychologist's or therapist's office—virtually wherever children are—for fun or learning or healing.

The ideas offered here are meant to trigger your ideas and are not intended to be a thorough list of all that can be done with or through puppets.

Puppets in the Home

In both home and school, children are more likely to use puppets if an example has been set by the adult. Parents can use puppets to advantage in teaching manners, to tell the bedtime story, to help with "talking time," to entertain at children's parties, and as a means of preparing a child for a new experience (role playing through puppets). Such new experiences might include a visit to the dentist, going on a trip, attending a birthday party, preparing for company, visiting a parent's work place, or practicing a talk to be given at school, such as "Show and Tell" or a book report. If the child is shy, perhaps the puppet can do the "Show and Tell" or book report.

With puppetry, every member of the family can be involved, if only as an appreciative audience. It is hoped that parents will view puppetry as a valuable skill their child can use for receiving needed recognition—a skill that can be used at school, camp, church, or club—wherever the need arises. For instance, a child who has seen a tree twig and a paper napkin turned into a stick puppet has a ready resource to entertain friends at camp. Imagination is used in a constructive rather than destructive way. The young child who demands undue attention when company is around might be encouraged to put on a puppet act as his or her contribution and thus get some recognition in a positive way.

Children who are sick in bed can entertain themselves with small hand or finger puppets, as can those confined to the back seat during a car trip. The wise parent of young children would do well to prepare a travel box or flight bag for all trips and excursions. This would contain small puppets, such as the finger puppets described in Chapter 9. What a holiday or birthday gift for a grandmother or aunt to prepare. One parent calls these the Dandy Handies and says, "When restlessness sets in, the puppet show begins."

Where puppets are available, children often entertain parents spontaneously with a quickie puppet skit. Parents who tape-record such skits acquire a record of their children's language development without making them self-conscious.

Puppets can enhance the parent–child relationship by providing a way to communicate when direct communication has broken down. A child, reluctant to talk about the school day, might be drawn out by the mother's use of a puppet. Or, not knowing how to relate an unpleasant experience to the family, a child might find the words through a puppet friend.

Parents might have a listening puppet, such as Lenny the Listener, whose sole role is being an active listener. He reflects back feelings but does no preaching, teaching, advising, or questioning. "Listening is loving," says author Bob Conklin, and this puppet is a real lover. The child may like to wear a "Tracy the Talker" puppet while talking. "Lenny the Listener" may become part of the bedtime ritual, a routine so important in the lives of young children.

Where prayers, thanksgiving, or affirmations are said at bedtime, a puppet may be used to lead the child in these or simply to listen to them. Puppets are particularly good for reinforcing affirmations through repetition.

Bedtime stories via a puppet are an obvious opportunity, but to encourage creativity, let the child tell the story some of the time, or use open-ended stories where the child can supply the ending. Another way to encourage creative thinking during stories is to ask questions occasionally, such as: What do you think will happen next? What do you suppose she saw? What would you have done if you were he? Such techniques are, of course, valuable in a group situation such as the classroom, where one child's thinking can stimulate another's.

Puppets can be a welcome addition to some family games. "Ungame," a noncompetitive board game, where players draw cards and share feelings and thoughts appropriate to the topic

47

selected, is a natural to play with puppets. Players can each assume the personality of the puppet they are using and respond accordingly, thus removing some of the pressure they might feel in answering for themselves. Holding two puppets at once or rotating puppets frequently can be an enjoyable challenge in this game.

Puppets in the School

The use of puppets begins in the nursery school, where they are invaluable when readily available for dramatic play. Teachers can teach finger plays with simple finger puppets, and hand puppets can act out familiar nursery rhymes. Music time is enhanced by a puppet leading the singing and other puppets joining in. The shy child who is reluctant to sing will often participate enthusiastically through a puppet. Puppets enjoy leading children in many "follow-the-directions" games; for instance, "Simon Says" can become "Puppet Says." They are also excellent for concept teaching and can help clarify abstract concepts and demonstrate concrete concepts. For instance, in the preschool, the concepts of *above, below, behind, in front of,* and so on can be clearly shown with the puppet. With older children, puppets can help illustrate concepts related to such areas as self-esteem, friendship, and creative thinking. The more important an idea is, the more the teacher might consider using a puppet to get it across.

At any grade level, teachers can find puppets a real aid in dealing with problems of social behavior. Children really recognize themselves in misbehaving puppets. For instance, if there is unpleasant recurring playground behavior, the teacher might have a group of students put on a puppet skit illustrating this.

Puppetry is a sure means of stimulating creative writing in older children or story telling with younger ones. Some teachers tape-record spontaneous puppet skits and, by writing them down, show the children how they have created a story. Open-ended stories, to be completed with puppets, also encourage creative thinking and writing.

48

Teachers find good use in puppets as icebreakers to relieve classroom tensions. Puppets just love to tell jokes and the latest riddles to children. They are also useful for informal quizzes. If children can't answer a question asked by a puppet, they don't feel as bad as when they can't answer an authority figure. If a child is responding with a puppet, it's his or her puppet that is stupid and not the child. Research concludes that oral reports of any type are usually easier for the shy child with the use of a puppet.

The retention of health and safety rules when taught by a puppet is impressive, as is the recall ability of any subject taught with the use of a puppet. Three-year-olds remembered months later the safety rules the teacher's puppet told them about.

Teachers know there is value in interrelating the subject areas taught; what better way to link them than a class puppet play! All these subjects and more may be involved in a play: music, art, drama, math, sewing, history, carpentry, social studies, English, and citizenship. Such a play makes a good program for Parents' Night or to take to another classroom. What an esteem builder it could be.

Class parties are livened up by puppet plays. A variety show or circus theme is especially appropriate because it allows all the children to get into the act and express their individuality.

In a classroom with a climate of psychological safety and freedom, the youngsters are bound to come up with countless ideas for using their puppet friends.

Specific Suggestions for Classroom Puppetry

- Create a classroom puppet library—a collection of puppets available to the students at all times, to be borrowed and returned.

- Put together a puppet center—Puppet Stuff Box, prop box, and theater or two, available for children to use during free time.

49

• Give the children a choice between being involved in creative drama or dramatic play. Make it okay for half the class to prefer one and the other half the other.

• If some children enjoy making the puppets more than using them, or vice versa, allow for such individual preferences. All don't have to be doing the same thing.

• Provide a home for each child's puppet, a box in which the puppet can have additional costumes and props. Let the child fix it up to his or her own satisfaction.

• Consider having a specific puppet for each subject area. This puppet could remind the class that it's music time, for instance, and be used to give directions and explain new concepts. Also, if it's a bright puppet, it might help the teacher by giving math drills, spelling tests, or whatever its specialty is. If the puppet has trouble in a subject area, the children could teach it and straighten out its confusion.

• Transfer some of the responsibility for classroom discipline to the puppet. It can act as the signaler for quiet time or for paying attention, so that the teacher is not always in the position of reminding or reprimanding. Also, the puppet can be the moderator at class meetings where discipline problems are resolved.

• Puppets for praise are used in various ways by teachers. In one classroom, "Fanny Tastic" chooses one child each day to honor in some special way. In others, the praise puppet is an astute observer and ends the day with statements like, "I especially liked the way Rick helped Johnny clean up all the spilled paint."

• Self-introductions are more comfortably performed through a puppet. Children choose a puppet from the box, and then the puppet and child talk together to get acquainted. Then, going around the room, the teacher calls on the puppet to introduce its new friend to the class.

50

• Puppets as mood indicators are very popular with teachers. A kindergarten teacher uses paper-plate stick puppets with the following expressions for many of her "feeling" activities.

HAPPY

MAD

SURPRISED

SAD

The child chooses a puppet to use and then tells why he or she is feeling that way. "How do you feel when . . . ?" situations are proposed, and a child chooses a puppet to respond with. In some classrooms every child has a "happy" and "sad" puppet at his or her desk. It has a happy face on one side of the paper cup or plate head and a sad face on the other side. Feelings are indicated by the side that is revealed. A speech therapist has found them effective in controlling undesirable behavior. She says, "The simple act of turning 'Mr. Speech' from happy to sad has accomplished more than any amount of nagging."

• A Surprise Box Puppet is popular in one primary classroom. Each week it is responsible for bringing something new and interesting to its surprise box. Sometimes the "Twenty Questions" game leads up to revealing the surprise.

• Felt boards and puppets work well together. A puppet with hands can effectively help the adult put pieces on or take them off the felt board. One teacher who was teaching toddlers the parts of the face used a rather stupid puppet that kept goofing up and putting the parts in the wrong place. The children had a lot of fun correcting it.

• Phonics puppets are really successful in kindergarten classrooms. The teacher has one for each letter, and the puppet can only say words beginning with its letter, or eat foods starting

51

with its letter. "Larry Lion loves licking licorice lollipops." Andy Alligator brings an apple, avocado, and asparagus for the children to taste.

- Puppets enliven science experiments by discussing them or performing simple ones. Puppets can be used in the natural sciences to represent the elements involved in a particular environment, such as a chemical compound, air, or water.

- Music teachers find that puppets help students develop a feeling for rhythm and music interpretation through moving the puppets to the beat. They also encourage reluctant children to sing, as the puppet does the singing and not the child. Puppets with moving mouths are most effective but not necessary. One preschool teacher had great success getting shy children to sing through decorated toilet-paper tubes that represented the mouths of animals.

- Social studies is a natural area for puppets; they present countless opportunities to dramatize historical events, represent particular cultural groups being studied, or portray the roles of various community helpers.

- Reading via a puppet brings results. One special-education teacher found that her students who disliked reading were able to read a little more easily and more happily with a puppet on the hand.

These suggestions are simply intended to be idea starters. The use of puppets in the classroom is only as limited as the teacher's attitude and imagination.

Puppetry Elsewhere

Puppets in the Sunday School

In some Sunday schools, the primary teachers have three puppets that are constantly used in various instructional lessons. They are Positive Posy (a flower), Negative No (a grey cloud), and Super Soul (a sun). These puppets portray various aspects of the personality and help the children become aware of their relationship with themselves and others.

Lou Austin's books *The Little Me and the Great Me* and *My Secret Power* have been used successfully by primary school teachers. The puppet learns to blow out the "Little Me" and breathe in the "Great Me." In these stories and others, the puppet serves as a convenient transition aid, after which the children move comfortably into applying spiritual principles directly to themselves.

One puppeteer teacher dramatically portrayed the Soul through a conversation between two hand puppets. He shook the puppets off his hands to reveal the Soul, and the two hands went on conversing. Bare hands used by a talented puppeteer can be so "alive." We really miss the boat if we think we need elaborate and detailed puppets.

Acting out Bible stories and reciting Bible verses is a popular use of puppets. Here, of course, they are only aids to memorizing information rather than the means for releasing creative thinking.

Puppets in Other Areas

Librarians have long had an affinity for these little man-made actors who are so effective at storytelling. The preschool story hour is often enlivened by the imaginative use of a puppet or two, who may talk about the stories before and after they are read or even actually tell or read a story. Puppets are so useful for keeping children's attention focused and for leading group discussions.

Many libraries have puppetry workshops, where school-age children get to make instant and inexpensive puppets and then put on plays for each other or the public. The children learn to create original stories or adapt classic stories; they become familiar with manipulation, characterization, and the other elements of drama. A permanent puppet stage and collection of ready-made puppets make a valuable addition to any library program.

Counselors' and therapists' offices are especially pro-

The Use of Puppets in the Home, School, and Elsewhere

ductive places for "puppet people," including whole families of puppets (father, mother, brother, sister, grandparents). Knowledge can come from feelings as well as feelings from knowledge, and puppetry is a superb way to get those feelings out, look at them, and learn from them under the guidance of a professional.

Puppets can be of most valuable assistance in the children's hospital. Rothenberg says that there are six questions that are always present in the hospitalized child's mind, although seldom explicitly stated:

- What do I have?

- How did I get it?

- Why did I get it?

- Will I get well?

- When will I get well?

- Why did my parents leave me in the hospital?

These questions have to be answered more than once, because the answers undergo some distortion as they are filtered through the patient's defense mechanisms.

A puppet dialogue is valuable here. The child's puppet will more freely ask the troubling questions, and the adult's puppet can respond as a comforting friend rather than an awesome health professional.

Some hospitalized children withdraw as a reaction to fear, anger, guilt, and sadness and might mistakenly be considered well-adjusted patients. Puppetry is an excellent device to draw out this type of child. Through the puppet, the child can act out his or her anger instead of becoming immobilized, express sadness instead of withdrawing, and get in touch with any guilt feelings. Another type of child acts out the fear, anger, guilt, and sadness and is labeled a "bad" patient. A puppet can express these feelings more constructively and safely for the child, because it is the puppet that is saying and doing all those awful things. It is important to provide the child with two puppets, so that all the hurt, anger, and fear can be lashed out between them. The more nondescript their faces and costumes, the more they can be whatever the patient wishes them to be.

We have only begun to realize the educational and therapeutic possibilities of puppetry.

7

Puppet Manipulation and Characterization

Puppetry is acting with your hands. Some say it is <u>thinking</u> with your hands. This makes movement the most important part of puppetry. It is through movement that the puppet is brought to life. It can only have as much life as the puppeteer gives it.

As important as voice may be, it is not essential to puppetry. In some countries puppet shows are performed entirely through movement because of language barriers.

The type of movement depends on the type of puppet being used, but here we are going to concentrate on the hand puppet with hands, since it can do more than all the others and is usually preferred by young children.

The puppeteer should keep in mind that a puppet can do things even people can't, such as fly or remove its head. Encourage the child to think about all the things a puppet might do other than just wiggle.

Here is a list of some of the things these man-made actors can do. Lead the child to think about what actions would indicate these activities. It would be good exercise to practice each of these until the movements are perfected:

walk	think	pick up things
march	cry	lie down
dance	hit	fall down
sneeze	write	wash hands
climb	push	sit down
limp	search	rise
nod	point	look behind
bow	pray	act frightened
wave	scratch	remove hat
clap	eat	lead songs
yawn	laugh	play music
throw kiss	brush hair	brush itself off
carry	hammer	die
scrub	read	come to life
sweep	fly	sleep
swim	gallop	wake up
kneel	scold	take head off
skip	do exercises	put head on

Two children together might enjoy practicing the things puppets can do in pairs, such as:

shake hands
embrace, kiss
chase one another
fight
dance together

talk together
hand objects back and forth
carry something together
have a tug-of-war
play catch

There are additional exercises at the end of this chapter.

It is considered best to practice in front of a mirror that is positioned so that just the puppet is seen and not the puppeteer.

Some books, such as Engler and Fijan's, give excellent, detailed, step-by-step directions for basic puppet movements. Others favor original spontaneous actions.

The Prop Box

The next logical step is practicing with props from the prop box.

This box should always be readily available for whenever a prop is needed. A search through the drawers and cupboards of your home will turn up a vast variety of articles that puppets can find imaginative ways to use. They should be oversized in relation to the puppet to make them easier to see and handle and more humorous. Just about anything can be included—boxes and books to open, hats to wear, flags to wave, containers to put things in, brooms for sweeping, and ropes to pull for a tug-of-war.

61

Have the puppet practice all the things that can be done with any particular prop, including picking it up, putting it down, dropping it, and so on. One exercise for students is the extemporaneous skit with assigned props. The adult distributes slips with such directions as, "Using two puppets and these props (mirror, basket, pencil), do a three-minute skit."

As to the talking type of hand puppet, one should be aware that it can do much more than just talk. Puppeteers can begin by looking in the mirror and seeing how many things they can do with their own mouths and then can practice making their puppet smile, frown, spit, sputter, cough, sneeze, bite lips, and lick lips.

And the finger puppet with legs can do more than walk. It can kneel, kick, skip, jump, tap its toe, dance, climb, march, hop, and run.

For hand puppets, some puppeteers suggest regular exercises, either with or without puppets, to keep the hands limber and improve manipulation.

Worrell suggests using the puppet on stage and going through a specific series of movements briefly summarized here:

1 Up-and-Down Bobbing Movements.

The puppet first walks with short up-and-down bobbing movements, then with an up-and-over movement like hopping or leaping. This is almost like drawing circles in the air. Next it bobs up and down very fast as though running from a tiger, and then up and down slowly as though it is worn out from running.

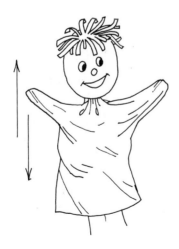

2 Twisting Around-and-Back Movements.

Move the puppet across the stage, twisting your wrist around and then back as you go. Repeat this using small, fast, twisting movements, and then do it with large, slow twists. Next try large but fast twists to give the appearance of a frantic run. If the puppet has long hair, it will fly and flip. Then try small and slow twists to make a dainty walk.

3 Back-and-Forth Rocking Movement.

As the puppet walks, have it rock forward, then backward, forward, then backward. If this is done quickly, it appears to take very small, quick steps. When done with large, slow movements, it looks as though it is taking large steps. Try moving it up and down at the same time it goes back and forth. Try leaning it forward as it rocks like a very old person or backward like it might be "stuck-up." As it walks, have it look at the ground for something or at the sky.

4 Side-to-Side Swaying Movement.

Take the puppet across the stage, having it lean first to its left, then to its right. Have it sway side to side with large movements that lean it way over. Do it slowly first, then fast. Next have the puppet use very small side-to-side swaying movements. Do it quickly to get a nervous kind of walk. Moving the puppet up and down as it sways from side to side gives the impression of a limp.

5 Combining Arm and Walking Movements.

Once the foregoing basic walking movements are learned, practice using arm movements along with them. Push or pull with the arms, swing them, bring them together over the stomach and back out to the side, and so forth.

65

Since performing with puppets can be physically tiring, you might want to consider these simple exercises suggested by Philpott (1967, p. 21) as a means of building up strength:

Hold one of your arms above your head for five minutes, then relax. Then hold both arms in front of you at waist level, bent at the elbows. Keep this position for five minutes and then relax. Now repeat the exercises holding some kind of weight in each hand. One quickly becomes aware of the importance of puppets being light weight.

Creegan recommends doing the following hand exercises at eye level daily:

1 Opening and closing hands rapidly, stretching the fingers way out and then closing them—twenty times.

2 Revolving each finger in a circle, keeping the rest of the hand stationary—twenty times.

3 Finger push-ups. The hand is pressed against the wall and raised with the strength of the fingers—ten times.

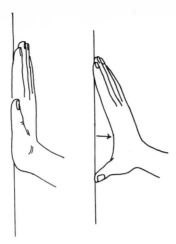

A particularly good exercise for children that requires the use of imagination, as well as muscles, is to have them practice walking the puppet in all different manners—as a duck, kangaroo, rabbit, turtle, squirrel; as a tired, infirm person; a happy, sprightly person; a stately, sad person; and so forth. They should learn that a puppet reveals its personality through its walk.

Inexperienced puppeteers tend to wiggle the puppet, wave the arms, and allow the puppet to lean forward at an unnatural angle. These faults can be overcome through practice and watching the puppet. Good puppeteers never take their eyes off their puppets. When working with children, however, one may need to keep one eye on the puppet and one on the children.

The puppet's gestures should be exaggerated so as to be easily recognized and to make an emotional impact. There is a rule that only the puppet speaking has the action. Slight movements of the head indicate which puppet is talking while the others remain motionless. But they should appear alert and interested, not drooping or frozen.

Even though the puppet has just one facial expression, it can give the impression of having changed it by changing its position. For instance, if it is mad, it can turn its back angrily. If sad, it can hang its head or slouch.

Hand puppets excel at picking up things. To make them even more effective, sometimes magnets are sewn in the palms.

Puppets make more effective entrances and exits if they come in from the side of the stage instead of just popping up or dropping down.

YES!

NO!

After the mechanical control of the puppet is well in hand, it is time to work on characterization. The personality of each puppet should be decided upon, and this should be kept consistent in terms of voice and actions. The character of the puppet can be established for just one play or situation, or it can be set for all time. Some families or classrooms have puppets that never change character, and they develop real personalities that can be counted on always to behave in certain ways—bossy, selfish, shy, generous, greedy, lying, know-it-all, hostile, affectionate, and so forth. They become authentic group members whose personalities affect the group.

Once the personality of a puppet is established, its voice, movements, and clothing easily follow. Children should be encouraged to costume their puppets in ways that make each one just right for its role. Just the kind of hat and the way it is worn can be a clue to character.

The voice chosen should agree with the physical appearance of the puppet—frail, sickly man, a quavery voice; a witch, a nasal cackle. Beginners sometimes mistakenly make the voice tiny and squeaky just because the puppet is tiny. Also, many err in speaking too fast and letting the voice drop at the end of a sentence so that it is inaudible. Because it is harder to understand a person's speech when you can't watch the face and lips while he or she talks, it is very important to have the puppet speak clearly and loudly. Tricks for changing one's voice include speaking into a tin can, holding the nose, and using an accent.

68

One can sharpen characterization by giving each puppet mannerisms—distinctive behavior traits—such as the repeated use of certain gestures or phrases. Characters in a puppet play should be one of a kind, each strikingly different from the others to avoid confusion.

> "On sensitive hands, puppets
> can live, but they demand
> more than your hands—you
> must give them your heart."
>
> Tom Tichenor

Additional Puppet Exercises

Remember to practice before a mirror as much as possible.

1 Practice everything that each of the following animals can do: cat, dog, mouse, rooster, horse, lion, elephant, crow, goat, seal, a make-believe animal, and so forth. Do not forget their voices. Each exercise can be preceded by a group discussion of the things that animal can do. For instance, a dog can pant, yelp, whine, bark, growl, scratch itself, dig for a bone, sit up and beg, run, jump up on a person, search, get ready to sleep.

2 Practice all the ways people can move, using various types of puppets.

3 Discover and practice all the things a puppet can do that a real person or animal cannot do. This is where the magic of puppets comes in.

4 Practice all the ways that people use their voices. An easy way to get started is simply to practice high and low voices with two different puppets. A puppeteer can work alone, or two can work together with one asking questions in a low voice and the other answering in a high voice.

5 Choose different voices, and play a guessing game with a partner, taking turns guessing who the voices represent. Some voices that can be used for practice are Santa Claus, a witch, a small child, a weepy person, an excited person, a sleepy person. To get familiar with voices used in different ways, suggest that the children close their eyes during a Saturday cartoon show on TV.

6 Play the "mirror" game, where one puppet reflects back the motions of the other. This may be played by two children or by one child and two puppets.

7 Try these puppet actions without props:

lift something heavy, light
drive a car fast, slow
sit down, lie down
stumble, fall down
act angry, throw something
search for something
scratch ear, nose, head
pour tea, drink it
act physically hurt

bounce a ball
wash a window
do exercises
cry, cover eyes
rock in a rocking chair
set the table
make, cook pancakes
pick flowers, berries
play the piano

Add your own ideas.

70

8 Work with another puppet (two puppeteers may pair up, or one may work with two puppets), and do the following:

whisper together	dance together
comb other puppet's hair	comfort crying puppet
spank other puppet	teeter-totter together
paint a wall together	use as many of the props as
spar or wrestle	possible as a team

9 Play an action guessing game with other puppeteers. Each thinks of two or three clear-cut movements that his or her puppet then performs onstage. For instance, the puppet might enter bouncing a ball, lose it, and run offstage after it. If the audience is unable to understand what the puppet is doing, the puppeteer explains. Part of the practice can be the puppet actor's carefully entering and leaving the stage.

10 Play charades with puppets. The puppet acts out a secret word for the audience to guess, such as *whirl, stumble, fly, leap, knock, exercise, run, bow, bounce, sleep, dance,* and so on. These individual words can be written on slips of paper and distributed to the students for practice ahead of time.

11 Play the popular "Simon Says" game, with the leader's puppet being Simon, or Bozo, or whatever the puppet's name is. The children follow the leader with their hand puppets and are eliminated if their puppet makes a sound or performs an action that Simon didn't say to do.

12 "Talk with Your Hands." Using just your bare hands as puppets, pantomime as many actions and emotions as you can.

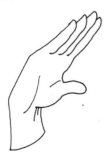

Puppet Manipulation and Characterization

8

The Puppet Stuff Box

The magic of puppetry starts with a puppet stuff box. This permanent box of possible puppet materials serves as a ready resource for creating puppets whenever one has the desire and time to make them. Motivation can quickly fall away for adult and child alike if too much time has to be spent in collecting the materials needed.

The most unlikely odds and ends can make the most intriguing puppets. Include things from the beach, the woods, and most any room in the house. Children should be encouraged to add to the puppet stuff box and helped to discover new uses for seemingly useless things. Not all the materials in this magic box should be throwaways. It is wise to keep on hand some semi-prepared puppet heads for the times when someone has a spur-of-the-moment idea. Discarded heads of small dolls are good for this. Materials for clothing, wigs, and facial features should be readily available, so that the moment of inspiration is not lost while having to hunt high and low.

Include in the puppet stuff box a small box of basic equipment: scissors, masking tape, glue, needle and thread, pins (straight and safety), rubber bands, paper fasteners, string, felt pens, crayons, pipe cleaners. In a school situation, the teacher might have several such boxes to be checked out from her desk. The puppet stuff box will be more appealing if items are neatly arranged in it in smaller boxes or bags. For instance, all wig material could be together, all felt scraps in another bag, sticks tied together, and so on.

Here are some of the items that can help create magic for children:

- sticks for stick puppets (paint sticks, chopsticks, dowels, tongue depressors, straws)

- Styrofoam balls of all sizes, hollow rubber balls

- discarded doll heads, socks, torn nylon stockings

- gloves, mittens, fabric scraps large enough for costumes, old bed sheets

- felt scraps for facial features, shirt sleeves for costumes

- old handkerchiefs, doll clothes, and little hats

- paper sacks and plates (all sizes), shirt cardboard

- envelopes (business and standard size), paper cups, Styrofoam cups, yogurt cartons

- construction paper, crepe paper, paper doilies, Jell-O and pudding boxes, egg cartons, paper towel tubes, Big Mac boxes, boxes of various sizes

- plastic bottles of all shapes and sizes (bleach, detergent, etc.)

- wig materials (yarn, fur scraps, scouring pads, feathers, and the like)

- buttons, beads, sequins, discarded jewelry, old lace, trim, iron-on tape scraps, balloons, wooden spoons, spools, fuzzy slippers, sponges, jar lids, Ping-Pong balls, old toys or toy parts, cotton batting, cotton balls, kitchen utensils, fly swatters, hair brushes, toilet brushes

- whatever else your imagination recognizes or discovers.

Occasionally, include some "way-out" articles. The more unusual, the more the child's thinking will be challenged. A bicycle tire pump? A stethoscope? A whisk broom?

The children will enjoy decorating the puppet stuff box to indicate its magical contents.

9
Making
Instant
Puppets

How the puppet is made is not as important as <u>what</u> is done with it. The emphasis here is on instant puppets that don't take long to make, thus allowing more time for their use. The values of puppetry for young children that were discussed earlier will not be realized if most of the time is spent making the puppet instead of using it.

Imagination is the most important ingredient in puppet making. Experimentation and original ideas are to be encouraged, always keeping in mind that the puppet should be a product of the <u>child's own</u> imagination and experience. Sometimes a teacher keeps a scrapbook of pictures of animals and of people in various costumes as a quick reference for older children.

There are two basic approaches to creating the puppet:

- Make it, and decide on use later..

- Decide on use, and then make it.

It is recommended that before making a puppet, the children first think of the use to which it will be put. If this is not known, they can at least think about the sort of character to be made. Is it to be pleasant or grouchy? Wise or stupid? Shy or aggressive? Rich or poor? The puppet's personality can unfold during the process of making it if the maker begins a dialogue with the puppet through thoughts or words.

Stick, hand, and finger puppets are emphasized in this section, because they offer the most possibilities for "all-of-a-sudden" puppets (except, of course, for invisible puppets).

Stick Puppets

Any two- or three-dimensional figure or head attached to a slim, rigid support can become a stick puppet. Some of the types of sticks used as the control rods for these puppets are: doweling, rulers, lengths of bamboo, tree branches, tongue depressors, Tinkertoy sticks, Popsicle sticks, clothespins, chopsticks, and paint paddles.

Paper Figure Puppets

This type of instant puppet is made of paper figures. It is preferable that they be drawn by the child but they can also be cut out of paper doll books, coloring books, catalogs, or inexpensive storybooks and then taped to a stick. Cardboard backing makes for a more durable puppet. Flat-face puppets are a variation of this. Here the child paints or pastes a face on a cardboard circle or paper plate, which is then fastened to a flat stick.

Tongue Depressor Puppets

This type of puppet is closely related to the paper figure puppets and is great for children who can handle scissors and enjoy drawing. Two construction paper heads are cut out at the same time and glued or stapled together to form an envelope. The top of a tongue depressor is then inserted into the open end, leaving about three inches for the hand to hold.

The child can design face and hair from construction paper scraps or use felt pens. A happy face can be made on one side and a sad face on the other to represent the puppet's moods, or two entirely different characters can be represented on the two sides. Wrap-around clothing made from construction paper, metallic foil, or fabric scraps can be added.

Paper-Bag Stick Puppets

These puppets begin with a piece of doweling about an inch thick stuck into a lunch-sized paper bag that the child has stuffed with torn newspaper. The stick is best held in place by string or masking tape wrapped tightly around the end of the sack. The child then glues on either felt or construction paper facial features, ears, and hair. Felt pens or paint also work well. Older children may wish to dress the puppet with a fabric square or old shirt sleeve large enough to cover the hand.

Spoon Puppets

Spoon puppets are usually made with wooden spoons and can be quite charming. The handle becomes the control rod, and the bowl serves as the face, which can be decorated with felt pens or colored construction paper. Facial features can also be made with gummed-back shapes such as stars and paper reinforcers. A copper scouring pad can be glued on for interesting hair, or scraps of fake fur or yarn can be used to create a wig. A construction paper hat or bonnet can be slipped over the spoon head in lieu of hair. Again, this stick puppet can be dressed or not, depending on age and ability of the child. Very similar to the spoon puppet is the lollipop puppet, which is made in the same way from a large lollipop.

Styrofoam Stick Puppets

Styrofoam puppets are made by sticking the sharpened end of a dowel or any other kind of stick into a Styrofoam egg or ball. Felt, buttons, or beads for facial features can be stuck on with tiny straight pins or glue. Smaller Styrofoam balls cut in half are great for ears, noses, and cheeks. An old nylon stocking stretched tightly over the head can give color to the face. An instant way of dressing this puppet is to put a nine-inch square of fabric over the stick and thrust the covered end into the ball.

Fruit and Vegetable Stick Puppets

Such stick puppets might be consumed at a birthday party or picnic, or they might end up in soup or salad when the play is over. Use a large carrot as is, or simply insert a stick (such as a tongue depressor) into the bottom of a potato, apple, orange, cucumber, or the like. To conceal the hand, fasten a cloth around the top of the stick with a pipe cleaner or bread-wrapper twist. Design the face with such items as tacks, toothpicks, raisins, small marshmallows, gumdrops, cloves, buttons, ribbon, and jewelry. Pipe cleaner arms and legs can be added, if desired.

Envelope Stick Puppets

These can be the most instant stick puppets of all. Simply put a ruler in the slit end of a sealed legal-sized envelope, and draw a figure on it. Felt pens or crayons can make a colorful figure, or construction paper can be pasted on to form the clothing.

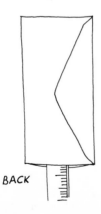

BACK

FRONT

FRONT

Household Object Puppets

The household object puppet comes from the toolbox, broom closet, kitchen drawer, wherever. Extraordinary puppets can be made with the most ordinary household items, great sources for this "spur-of-the-moment" puppet. Look with fresh eyes at such items as egg beaters, toilet bowl brushes, spatulas, hammers, wrenches, feather dusters, funnels, paper bowls, jar lids, strainers, plastic detergent and bleach bottles, margarine tubs, hair brushes, old slippers, clothespins, and even paper napkins. Puppets are where you find them! One imaginative preschool teacher shaped a very large sponge with scissors, glued on a face, dressed it appropriately for each season, and used it regularly for discussions and story telling.

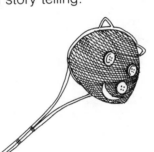

HANGER AND HOSE PUPPETS This type is made by stretching a nylon stocking leg over a wire coat hanger that is bent into the shape of an elongated head. Different head shapes can be tried.

FRINGE

The stocking is gathered at the bottom of the head and fastened with a pipe cleaner or other "twister." Facial features from felt or paper scraps are glued on as well as hair from yarn, fake fur, or construction paper.

THE CARDBOARD TUBE PUPPET   Since cardboard tubes are so readily available in the household (from toilet paper, paper towels, aluminum foil, plastic wrap, etc.), it is easy to make them part of the child's puppet inventory.

There are several ways of recycling these tubes as puppet characters. The tube can become just the face part of the puppet, with a cloth or paper "body" covering the hand. Or the entire tube can become the puppet body with a Styrofoam head glued to the top. Or, usually the easiest, the tube is made to represent both face and body of the puppet.

Construction paper can be cut to fit around the cardboard roll, or the tube can be used as is with facial features and clothing added by using felt or paper scraps, felt pens, or paint. In addition to construction paper strips, hair can be made from yarn, pot scrubbers, tissue paper, or feathers. Hats are a natural for these puppet people. Pipe cleaner arms could be added, but are not necessary.

These tubes used horizontally also make a fun variety of animals. Both adult and child can exercise their imaginations with very little expense.

The tube puppet can become a hand puppet rather than a stick puppet by wrapping fabric near the base of the tube and holding the tube under the fabric with the last three fingers, while using the thumb and index finger for hands.

THE CHRISTMAS BALL PUPPET   This is also known as the "See Yourself Puppet." It requires a shiny Christmas tree ball in which you can see your reflection, some masking tape, wire, and enough cloth to cover the hand. Wrap a length of wire around the ring on the ornament, and form a stem. Cover the wire with the tape, poke a hole in the center of the cloth, and pull the wire through it. Hold the puppet by the stem inside the cloth.

One teacher calls this her crystal ball puppet and uses it as a discussion starter. For example, the children look into it and see themselves doing something they have always wanted to do, and then they tell about it. Or they may see themselves in an especially happy place or in a place that frightened them or when they are grown up.

Shadow Puppets

Closely related to stick puppets are instant shadow puppets. The simplest are nonjointed stiff cardboard cutouts, but paper fasteners can be used for making a jointed puppet. As with the stick puppets, coloring book characters, paper dolls, and felt board figures can be used. A cardboard backing may be needed.

89

There is, of course, no need to worry about costuming. A stiff wire can be bent and taped to the back of the figure to make a good holder.

A quick and easy screen on which to project the shadows is a white bed sheet pinned over a cord hung like a clothesline or it can be tacked across a doorway. A small screen can be made by putting wax paper or a white trash-can liner in the cutout bottom of a sturdy dress box. The bottom is then placed upright in the lid of the box, and the puppets are worked behind the screen. A couple of wrapped bricks set inside the lid will hold the screen in place.

Another simple shadow screen can be made in similar fashion by cutting through a carton diagonally and cutting a stage hole on the front side (see drawing). A gooseneck desk lamp with a strong bulb makes for good lighting.

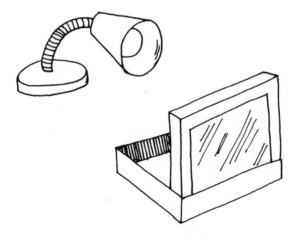

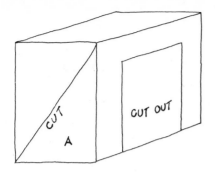
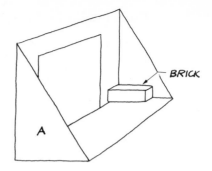

In the classroom, the overhead projector is a lot of fun to use for small shadow puppets. Just move them around on the projector, and watch the show on the screen. This can be quite educational visually. Paper clips bent in an L-shape and taped on the back of the figures provide an easy way to move these puppets around. Another fun medium to use is foam rubber sheeting, available in crafts shops. It can be cut into silhouettes and placed on the lighted overhead projector, as with cardboard cutouts.

The light of a slide projector can be used to cast shadows on a screen, and exciting or humorous backgrounds can be achieved by the selection of slides projected, such as foreign places, country scenes, animals, and so forth.

The most instant shadow puppet of all is the hand shadow. Children very quickly pick up how to make dogs, rabbits, and other silhouettes with their hands, and the bibliography mentions books that further that ability.

Hand Puppets (Glove Puppets)

There are two basic types of hand puppets—those whose mouths move and those that have hands. Each type can be made with both paper sacks and socks. Usually puppets that "talk" are easiest for the very young child to work if they are not too big for the child's hand. The following instant hand puppets are classified according to basic material used.

91

Paper-Bag Puppets

Paper-bag puppets offer the advantage of easy accessibility of inexpensive materials and a variety of forms, from simple to complex, that can be made quickly with no sewing required. The bag is used in two basic ways—empty or stuffed.

The empty bag puppet can take two different forms:

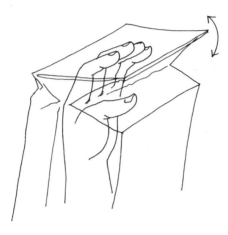

- the mouth can be on the bottom flap of the bag centering on the crease, so that when the flap is opened and shut, the mouth "speaks"

- the eyelids and eyelashes can be on the fold and the eyes themselves beneath the flap, so that moving the flap will open and shut the eyes.

One can use brown bags from the grocery store, white bags from the bakery, or brilliant-colored glazed bags from gift stores. Paper or fabric can be superimposed over the front of the bag to make clothing, or it can be drawn on with crayons or felt pens.

The second type of paper-bag puppet has a head stuffed with paper toweling or newspaper and usually has arms which are the puppeteer's fingers. Puppets of this type can range from simple one-bag puppets to complex two-bag puppets.

The one-bag puppet usually has a string or masking tape halfway down the bag to form the neck of the puppet. It is usually most satisfactory when a small cardboard tube is inserted in the bag and the neck string tied around it (see illustration). Holes near the front of the bag allow the fingers to become puppet hands. Face, hair, and clothing can be simply drawn or painted on, or such materials as crepe paper, fabric, yarn, buttons, and sequins can be used.

For a two-bag "person" puppet, a small bag, which is the head, is inserted in a hole in the bottom of a larger bag, which serves as the costume. The head bag is stuffed with newspaper, and a string is tied around it for the neck. The puppeteer holds onto the lower part of this bag, while at the same time using the thumb and index finger for puppet hands. It can be useful to wrap this part of the bag with masking tape as shown. Arms and legs, if desired, can be added by stapling or taping on more paper bags or by using whatever material is used for dressing the puppet.

94

Sock Puppets

Like paper-bag puppets, sock puppets can be either "talking" puppets or puppets with hands. They have the advantage of being tough, durable, flexible, and easily stored.

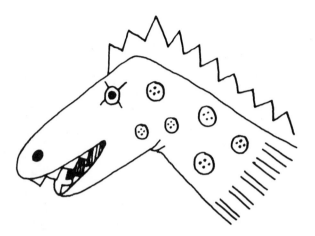

The quickest sock puppet is simply a sock put on like a mitten with two buttons added for eyes. Another quickie method is to poke the toe of the sock back into the hand and sew across the fold at each corner for the mouth. After tucking in the toe, it works best to have someone fasten tiny safety pins in the sides of the mouth. Then remove sock and sew. The sock should fit snugly on the hand with the heel at the top. The more flexible the mouth, the more expressive, so some puppeteers advise not lining it with felt.

The usual sock puppet is made by cutting around the edge of the toe and stitching or gluing in a piece of felt for the mouth. The felt is creased at midpoint so that four fingers are inserted above the mouth and the thumb is inserted below. Sometimes a piece of cardboard is glued on the back side of the mouth to give it more body. The puppet can, of course, be decorated in many ways. This is where the child's imagination should have free rein.

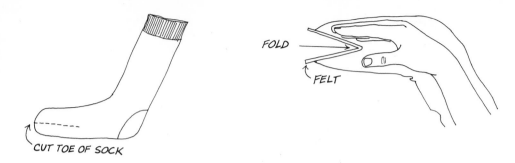

FOLD

FELT

CUT TOE OF SOCK

Felt can be used to make the basic ''talking'' sock puppet when socks aren't available. Use a modified sock shape, as illustrated, and some creativity to turn it into any number of animals.

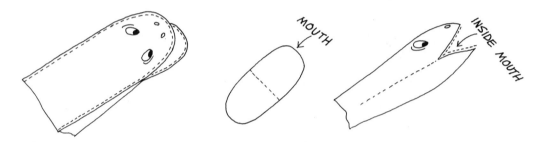

MOUTH

INSIDE MOUTH

The other basic type of sock puppet is made by stuffing the toe of a sock with soft material (nylon stockings, cotton, facial tissue) and tying it around the neck but leaving room to insert the index finger. Slits can be made for armholes and a costume created from fabric scraps. The Hopper book has good pictures of such costuming, and the Worrell book suggests many interesting techniques for making faces on sock heads.

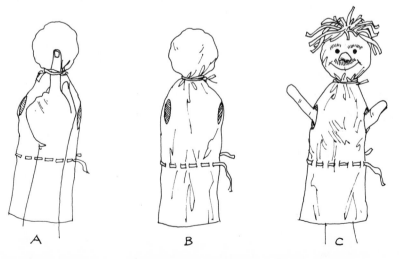

A   B   C

Yarn wigs are easily attached either by sewing on individual double strands or by making a simple wig of lengths of yarn stitched or tied across the center, which is then tacked onto the head with a few stitches or pins.

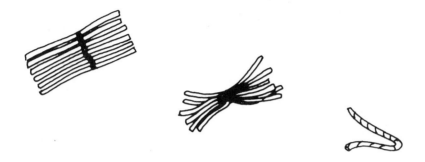

Styrofoam or Rubber-Ball Hand Puppets

These two types of hand puppets can be truly instant puppets, or they can be embellished and made quite elaborate. A hole is either hollowed out of the Styrofoam ball to fit the finger or cut in a hollow rubber ball. To make clothing, a large square of colorful fabric is draped over the index finger, which is inserted into the head. The handle of a spoon punches a good finger hole in Styrofoam. Slits in the fabric may allow the fingers to come through for hands, or else, without cutting the fabric, rubber bands can be used on the two fingers to make hands.

Another way of using the rubber band to make hands is to take a #16 size rubber band, put it on one extended finger, twist it in a figure 8 (∞) behind the puppet, and loop the other end over the other extended finger. Instant hands!

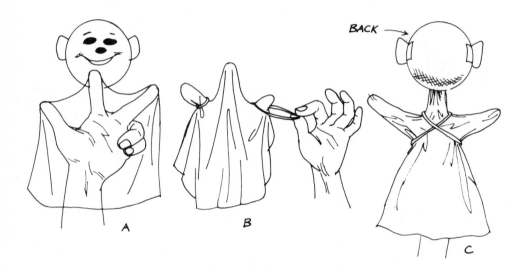

BACK

A

B

C

Another way of having instant hands is to simply use an old glove and stick the Styrofoam ball head on top of the index finger. The glove can be dressed up a bit, if desired.

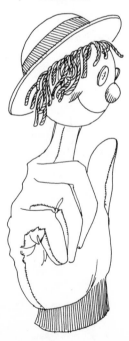

The rubber-ball head is best covered with the toe of a sock fastened on with a rubber band at the neck. This makes a good surface for gluing on facial features made from cloth scraps. With the Styrofoam head, the face can be made quickly by simply pinning on buttons, beads, sequins, or felt pieces. An old nylon stretched over the head can add color to the face, or rouge can be applied. Another puppet effect can be made by cutting a big slit in the rubber ball to make a movable mouth. Mouths can also be cut away from Styrofoam balls.

A favorite instant puppet head has facial features cut from magazine pictures and glued or pinned on a Styrofoam ball. It is good to have a box of pictures of eyes, noses, ears, mouths, and hair available to choose from.

If hair is desired, consider fur, fringe, yarn, crepe paper, ball fringe, cloth, or ribbon strips. The piece of fabric for the clothing can also be a large handkerchief or piece of old sheeting that the children have drawn on or decorated with glued-on bits of colored cloth and rickrack.

Fruit and Vegetable Puppets

Fruits and vegetables can make hand puppets as well as stick puppets. Using apples, oranges, pears, cucumbers, squash, or potatoes, make a hole in the bottom so that a cardboard tube may be inserted for the finger. A piece of fabric can be fastened to the tubing for clothing and hands made as already men-

tioned. Instead of the usual hair material, one might try grasses, leaves, carrot tops, or parsley. Let the imagination go wild with the face. A carved and dried apple head makes a marvelous old wrinkled face.

Kelp Head Puppets

The ball end of the long beach kelp can be cut off and dried for a very effective head. Enough of a neck should be left for clothing to be tied to it.

Borrowed Head Puppets

One of the most instant of puppets is that made with a discarded toy head. The puppet stuff box should have heads from broken dolls, bubble bath containers, and so on. Fabric can be stuck in the neck for clothing, or small doll dresses can be fastened to a neck tube.

Papier-Mâché Heads

Papier-mâché is a very versatile puppet material. It has the advantage of being soft and workable when moist, and hard and durable when dry. Most puppet books go into detail on both strip and pulp papier-mâché puppetry, but I don't feel the results are instant enough for inclusion here.

There is a new version of papier-mâché, however, that comes close to instant puppetry. This is a plaster-impregnated material called Dip'n Drape (or by other trade names) and is available in most hobby shops. You simply dampen it with a sponge and form or drape it over the puppet head form. It dries hard in a couple of hours and then can be painted. The puppet head form might be a Styrofoam ball, a balloon, modeling clay that is later removed, or a light bulb covered with foil (so that when the bulb is broken, no glass pieces can be removed from the inside). Dip'n Drape can be used over pieces of Styrofoam to make hands and feet. Its possibilities are truly fascinating.

Puppets from Foam Sheeting

Foam rubber sheeting, rubber cement, and felt pens are all that is needed for an older child to make this instant puppet. A pattern of the child's hand can be made on paper and then traced with felt pen onto the foam rubber. Cut out both the front and back together, making them 1 inch larger than the tracing. Brush rubber cement along the inside edges of each piece, let them dry two minutes, then press the back and front together. Clothes, hair, and facial features are drawn on with colored felt pens, or one can glue on fabric pieces.

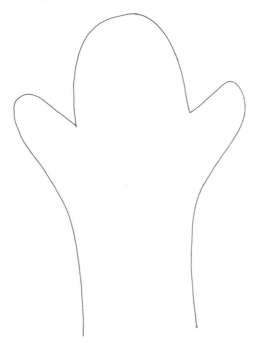

Cloth (Felt) Puppets

Similar to the foam-sheeting puppets is the "puppet glove" or cloth puppet, usually made with felt. One can cut two pieces of cloth as in the foam puppet directions and stitch or glue the edges together. Trim with buttons, rickrack, whatever's handy. Lightweight felt works nicely, and the features can be drawn, glued on, or stitched.

Mitten and Glove Puppets

Regular mittens can often be turned into interesting puppet people or animals with the addition of a little felt and yarn. Often mittens like this are available in the stores. Colorful garden gloves can be used just as they are with the use of some imagination. For instance, those printed with flowers, suns, or green bushes can be used by shy children who will only accept an inactive role in a puppet skit. This allows them to take part but not be under pressure to perform. A red glove has been used for Little Red Riding Hood along with a small basket on the thumb. A brown glove became the wolf and a white one, grandmother.

A marvelous spider puppet can be made from a black glove with a fat black pouch or puff attached to the back. Sew two large button eyes on this body pouch, and you have a scary spider to frighten Miss Muffet away.

Box Puppets

These "talking" puppets have the advantage of being made from easily obtainable scrap material—namely, gelatin, pudding, or miniature cereal boxes. The open ends of two boxes are taped together, so that four fingers go in the upper box and the thumb in the lower box. The boxes can be covered with paint, construction paper, or cloth scraps, and decorations can be added for the face. The costume may be a simple sleeve sewn or glued to the bottom box.

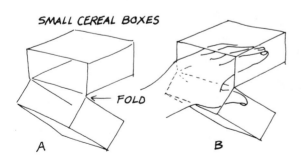

SMALL CEREAL BOXES

← FOLD

A

B

103

Paper-Plate Puppets

Along the same line as box puppets are paper-plate "talking" puppets. They are simple to make and take paint, crayon, and glue very well. A plain and sturdy paper plate is folded in half so that the outer rim of the plate forms the lips of a wide mouth. The fold makes the hinge that allows the mouth to open and close. Pockets into which the puppeteer slides his or her fingers can be made by stapling two paper plate halves to the top and bottom of the folded paper plate, leaving the back sides open. The fingers in the upper half and the thumb below make the mouth easy to operate. Teeth and tongues are fun additions to these puppets. A cloth sleeve attached to the plate can make the costume and hide the arm of the puppeteer.

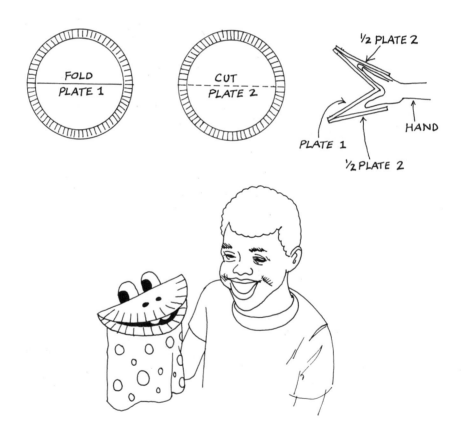

Envelope Hand Puppets

All that is needed to make an envelope hand puppet is a standard-sized envelope and a felt pen. Extras can be added, such as the construction-paper cone in the illustration.

Paper-Square Puppets

Another instant puppet is the paper-square puppet, which requires only paper, paste, scissors, and a stapler. A six-by-twelve-inch paper is folded in half, making a six-by-six-inch square. Two sides are stapled, leaving an opening on one side for the hand. To make the features, paper scraps can be curled, bent, twisted, cut, and pasted in countless ways.

105

Paper-Cup Puppets

Styrofoam cups work especially well for this type of puppet, but a paper cup will do. Make a hole in the cup for the nose, and poke the index finger through it. Eyes and mouth can be made with a felt marker or glued-on paper scraps or buttons. Paper strips make good hair, ears, whiskers, or what have you. Experiment with straws, pipe cleaners, toothpicks, and other objects. Three finger holes in a scrap of cloth make an instant costume.

Another good Styrofoam-cup puppet can be made by poking a hole in the bottom of a cup. Then, with a cloth draped over the hand, and cup held upright, push the index finger through the hole. Stuff colored tissue paper or other material into the cup for hair. A rubber band behind the puppet, shaped in a figure 8 over the fingers, will make instant hands. Or finger holes can be cut in the material. Facial features are drawn on with crayon or felt pen. One teacher had the children draw a Hesitant (fearful) Harry or Harriet on one side and a Happy Paulette (or Paul) on the other. Discussion centered around ways of making Hesitant feel better and less fearful.

106

Bare-Hand Puppets

One cannot leave hand puppets without mentioning the most readily available puppet of all——the kind that is drawn on the hand with a washable marker. One version is, with the fist clenched, to draw eyes on the hand and a mouth below the eyes and on the thumb. Another version is to draw a face in the creases of the child's palm. By moving the hand, one can create amusing expressions. Excellent examples of this type of puppet may be found in *Fun With Puppets* by Brody and Heron and in *Making Easy Puppets* by Shari Lewis.

Finger Puppets

The many advantages of these members of the puppet family were stated in Chapter 4, "Types of Puppets." Of the three types of finger puppets, my preference is for the ones with the finger legs because of their mobility and lifelikeness.

There are varying ways of making this type of puppet, but the most instant version is simply to cut the legs off a cardboard paper doll and tape a small rubber band at the lower back. The index and middle finger go through the rubber band to form legs. If desired, felt or paper can be added to the fingers to form shoes. Instead of using a paper doll, such a puppet can be made out of cardboard, felt, or stuffed cloth.

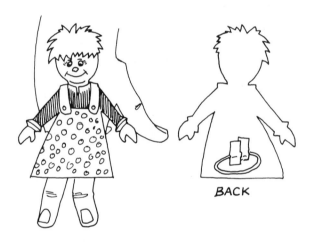

BACK

An effective variation is made by wearing an old glove with the index and middle fingers cut off. This makes the legs stand out, since the other fingers are concealed. In fact, a regular glove can be used with four fingers as the legs of an animal and the head of the animal attached to the middle finger of the glove.

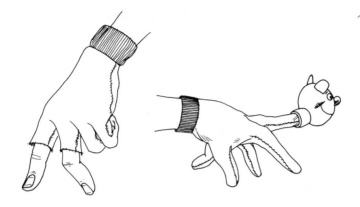

Another version of finger-leg puppet is made by drawing a puppet person and making two holes where the legs would go, then putting one's two fingers through these as legs.

The second category of finger puppets is the finger-cap type, which is manipulated with the puppeteer's fingers pointing upward. The many variations of this type are made by:

- Drawing faces on peanut shell halves.

- Cutting the fingers off a white work glove or other kind of glove and adding a felt pen face, paper ears, and so on.

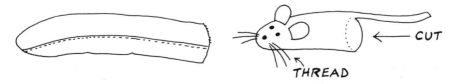

CUT

THREAD

• Using discarded miniature heads from toys.

• Making tubes from three-inch squares of felt rolled to fit the finger. Animal ears are best cut as part of the original square. Beads, sequins, and decorator braid can be used with imagination.

110

• Making construction paper cylinders to fit the finger and adding the puppet to this core. The head can be cut from a magazine or drawn by the child. The clothing can be a gathered piece of cloth glued onto the core or glued on construction paper or simply a felt pen design.

The third type of finger puppet, the finger-face, is discussed in Chapter 4.

Invisible Puppets

The invisible puppet can be the most instant puppet of all, except that it does require some thinking time.

Your puppet may appear out of thin air, or you may want it to have a permanent home of some sort where it will usually be found. This could be a little pillow, a shoe box fixed up like a house, a jar or can, a special pocket, a desk drawer, a window sill—almost anywhere.

As with all puppets, it is very important that it have a name and a definite personality. It need never talk unless you wish it to. You might be the only one who can hear what it says. If you, as the adult, set the pace with your invisible puppet, the children are sure to follow.

A variation of the invisible puppet is one of which just a little bit is visible, like just a pair of shoes or a hat. These could be operated by a string or a stick. How about making just a pair of magic glasses visible? A whole figure outlined by a wire shape could represent an invisible puppet. The puppeteer A. R. Philpott makes his heroine puppet invisible and portrays her actions with just his bare hand. Of course, other puppets can't see a human hand.

Invisible puppets are usually discovered somewhere. They may be found between the pages of a storybook, in an attic, in a tree, in a toy store, in a treasure chest, or wherever your imagination wants to find them. And they usually have such interesting experiences to relate!

111

Additional Puppet-Making Challenges

A Ten-Minute Puppet

This is a great imagination stimulator for yourself or older children. Beforehand, gather together scissors, glue, needle and thread, tape, and pins. Then go to one room in your house (kitchen, bathroom, bedroom, garage, anywhere) and, using only the materials you find there, make a ten-minute puppet. Set the timer, and really challenge yourself.

Nature Puppets

Go to the backyard or nearby park or beach, and see what kind of instant puppets you can make with the materials at hand. A real test of ingenuity.

Common Object Variations

A common object is assigned, and each person comes up with his or her version of a puppet based on this object. Possible objects are an apple, a carrot, a potato, an onion, a wooden spoon, an eggshell, a soda straw, a potato masher, a pancake turner, an old sack, a balloon, a peanut shell, a paper cup, an egg carton, a clothespin, a mirror, a milk carton, toilet paper tube, fork, bleach bottle, and so on.

Representational Puppets

A category is suggested, and the individual or group tries to come up with as many puppet ideas as possible in this category. Suggested categories might include a spider puppet, a butterfly puppet, a caterpillar puppet, a turtle puppet, a ghost puppet, a computer puppet, a fish puppet, a space traveler puppet, a bookworm puppet, and so on. An even harder challenge would be puppets to represent abstract ideas, such as peace, love, hate, truth, justice, and the like. Or how about puppets to represent music, sports, math formulas, chemicals, history? Don't rein in your imagination—try thinking of as many unusual ideas as possible for puppets.

Grab-Bag Puppets

Brown grocery bags are lined up. Into each of them the teacher puts a variety of ''puppet stuff''—enough to make a puppet or two. The bags are stapled shut and distributed at random to the students. The challenge is to create a puppet out of the items in the bag. Tape, scissors, and pins should be available.

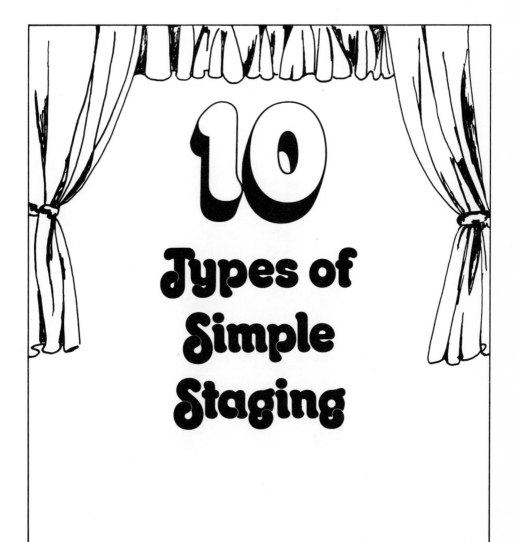

10

Types of Simple Staging

Simple staging devices are often the most satisfactory, because they are inexpensive, easily stored for later use, and readily disposed of following the play. There are two types of staging: one that allows the puppeteer to be seen and one that hides him or her from view.

Staging Where the Puppeteer Is Seen

1 It is possible to operate puppets with no stage at all, such as the Japanese Bunraku Puppet Theater does. One may prefer simply to sit at a table. That is perfectly all right, for audiences quickly forget about the puppeteer when captured by a puppet-actor.

2 An instant stage is the puppeteer's arm extended in front of him or her. The puppet just walks along the arm.

3 A purse or paper bag with a hole cut in the back makes a good staging device for a single puppet, because it usually takes the audience by surprise.

4 A large suitcase can open up into an instant stage and can be used to store puppets between performances.

5 A magic box is a small cardboard carton or hatbox with the back open and one or two holes in the top. It can sit beside the puppeteer or on a table in front of him or her. It can be decorated with colored paper, paints, or collage materials or be covered with contact paper, but it should not be so fancy as to detract from the puppets.

6 A big apron worn by the puppeteer with its corners lifted by two fellow puppeteers makes another ''all-of-a-sudden'' stage.

118

7 Some performers like to stand behind a draped table and hold in their free hand a large "mask" of a bush or tree to hide their faces.

8 A tray stage is a sturdy piece of cardboard bent at right angles and held by a strap around the neck. Two holes can be made in the bottom for hand puppets to appear through, or it can be used as is for finger puppets. Backdrop scenes can be sketched on the back of the stage or on paper and clipped to the stage.

9 Finger puppets can also be used through an opening cut in a cardboard box turned on its side. The simple box stages for shadow puppets, which are illustrated in Chapter 9, work fine for some finger puppets as well. Just remove the wax-paper screen.

The young child with the quiet voice is best off using a staging device where he or she is seen. Otherwise, the child's voice is easily muffled by the table top, blanket, carton, or whatever.

Staging Where the Puppeteer Is Not Seen

To make the puppet seem real and appear to be moving on its own, it is best to hide the puppeteer. Heightening this illusion of

119

reality is the main purpose of a puppet theater. The two kinds of theaters are:

- the puppet <u>booth</u> that has a window in which the puppets perform, and

- an <u>arena</u> theater that is open across the top.

10 A card table on its side or a sheet draped over a table makes a quick puppet stage for little ones.

11 A sheet or blanket thumbtacked across a doorway makes another "instant" theater. If using an old bed sheet, a scene may be spray-painted on it and slits cut in appropriate places for the puppets to pop out.

12 A similar idea is to use a tension-type curtain rod suspended across a doorway with a plain fabric curtain hung from it.

13 One may work over the top of a folding screen or wooden fence as do Jim Henson's television "Muppets."

14 The back of a sofa or a large cardboard carton can also be used in this way.

15 A large umbrella makes a great instant stage for small children.

16 A refrigerator carton makes a great puppet booth. A window is cut on one side and a door for entry into the box on the other side. A string across the inside top of the window will hold a curtain. Children can have a lot of fun painting a box like this with bright colors.

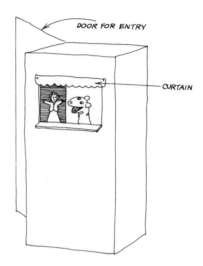

17 A table-top version of this puppet booth can be made from a smaller carton placed on a draped table. In this case, the back would be cut away, and there would be no door.

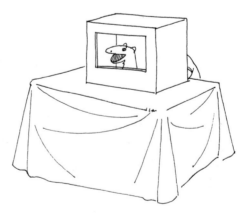

18 An old television cabinet can be cleaned out and used as a puppet stage for small-sized puppets.

19 Butcher paper can be stretched diagonally across a corner of a room, and a hole can be cut in it for a stage opening. A second piece stretched about twenty inches behind the first and a little above it can serve as a backdrop for scenery.

20 Pop-up hingelike windows can be made in large cardboard cartons that have been opened up like a folding screen.

21 The simplest permanent stage is the threefold hinged screen of a medium-weight plywood. It has a rectangular opening in the center section that is at the eye level of the audience and high enough to conceal the puppeteers. The outer panels, which are at right angles to the center panel, are kept in place by wire string above the top of the stage and about halfway back. It is held by eye screws and provides a line from which to hang backdrop scenery. Three scenes could be hung at one time and pulled across as needed. Some puppeteers prefer operating at chest level and so need a black, semitransparent curtain between them and the audience. They will not be seen if the lights

Types of Simple Staging

are stronger in front of the curtain than behind. Some kinds of cloth that are semitransparent are voile, sheer crepe, a cheap grade of velveteen, and some lining materials. Building instructions for this type of theater can be found in many books listed in the References. The *School Library Journal* of May 1977 has particularly detailed building instructions for this type of portable theater, and so does Worrell's book.

22 A table-top version of the foregoing theater is more portable and often more convenient for the adult. It is made lower, to sit on a table, and the puppeteer sits on a chair behind it.

23 Walking stages in which the puppeteer can perform as he or she moves from room to room in a hospital or school are pictured and described in the Worrell and Richter books. They are like moving puppet booths in which the puppeteer looks through semitransparent black material. A related idea is the large sombrero worn by one puppeteer. Dark fabric fastened to it conceals the puppeteer, who operates the puppets from a stage hole cut in the material.

24 Where possible, don't tie your puppets down to a stage. For instance, if you should decide to make a home movie of your puppet show, consider having the puppets appear in such places as a tree, a car, or on the roof.

Lighting

Some feel that the audience's attention should be focused on the stage by blotting out the immediate surroundings. This is done by darkening the room and spotlighting the puppets. This also puts everything on stage in scale and makes the puppets seem larger. A good inexpensive stage light is the ordinary clamp-on bed light. A gooseneck lamp trained on the stage also works, as does the beam from a slide or movie projector.

Music

When planning staging, keep in mind that music can help establish the mood of a puppet play. Piano, guitar, or even tape-recorded music at the beginning and end and during scene changes will give the show added appeal. You may wish to keep a notebook of musical themes or selections that would be appropriate for specific puppet situations. Sound-effect ideas might also be recorded in this booklet.

Conclusion

What is this magic of puppetry we've been talking about?

It is a world where children can be anything and everything they want to be, without fear or self-consciousness.

It is a world where imagination reigns supreme, because puppets have no mortal limitations.

Observing children in this magic world, the perceptive adult can discern their strengths and needs and can challenge them—appropriately—through the magic of puppetry.

A Word
on Praise
and
Appreciation

As children make and use puppets, we may be tempted to lavish praise on them, if we are not aware that praise can be destructive as well as productive. As Ginott points out in *Teacher and Child,* "Praise that evaluates is destructive and praise that appreciates is productive." Judgmental praise is to be avoided for a great many reasons, say Ginott and others, because it creates anxiety, invites dependency, and evokes defensiveness, among other things.

Barksdale, in *Essays on Self-Esteem,* also makes a strong case against this kind of praise. He says that probably the most destructive characteristic of this kind of praise is that it identifies the child with his actions. Such praise says that you are "good" because of your "good" acts, so the inference is that you are "bad" any time you make a mistake or act "bad." Such praise, Barksdale says, ignores or invalidates one's inherent worth and importance and implies that one must prove one's worth, that is, validate oneself through others' approval of one's conduct and accomplishments.

In *Your Child's Self-Esteem,* Dorothy Briggs says it this way, "Whenever personal worth is dependent upon performance, personal value is subject to cancellation with every misstep."

Appreciation is the constructive type of praise that builds self-esteem instead of tearing it down. It is simple recognition or observation of a constructive act and nonjudgmental appreciation of its consequences. It describes the child's performance and our feelings about the accomplishment, but it does not judge. Appreciation separates the deed from the doer, the act from the actor. Our appreciation is shown for the act or the deed. The evaluation of the child is left up to the child alone.

Dorothy Briggs suggests avoiding judgmental praise by telling youngsters what is going on inside you. She recommends using ''I'' statements rather than ''you'' statements to show appreciation. For instance, ''I enjoy your puppet performances'' is preferable to ''You're a good puppeteer''; ''I think that puppet is just beautiful,'' preferable to ''You have so much artistic talent.''

This form of praise acknowledges the innate worth of the individual by separating the person from his or her actions.

As you involve children in the magic of puppetry, you will have countless opportunities to appreciate their deeds. Just remember to keep the emphasis on the deeds and not the doer.

References

Puppetry Books

Many of these books are now out of print, but they are still very valuable resources and are available through the library system.

Adair, Margaret Weeks. *Do-It-In-A-Day Puppets: For Beginners.* New York: John Day, 1964.

————, and Elizabeth Patapoff. *Folk Puppet Plays for the Social Studies.* New York: John Day, 1972.

Andersen, Benny E. *Let's Start A Puppet Theater.* New York: Van Nostrand Reinhold, 1973.

Arnott, Peter D. *Plays Without People.* Bloomington IN.: Indiana University Press, 1964.

Baird, Bill. *Art of the Puppet.* New York: Macmillan, 1966.

Batchelder, Marjorie H. *Puppet Theater Handbook.* New York: Harper & Row, 1947.

————, and Virginia Lee Comer. *Puppets and Plays: A Creative Approach.* New York: Harper & Row, 1956.

Bates, Enid, and Ruth Lowes. *Potpourri of Puppetry: A Handbook for Schools.* Belmont, CA.: Fearon Publishers, 1976.

Beresford, Margaret. *How to Make Puppets and Teach Puppetry.* New York: Taplinger, 1966.

Binyon, Helen. *Puppetry Today.* New York: Watson-Guptill, 1966.

Blackham, Olive. *Puppets into Actors.* New York: Macmillan, 1949.

Bodor, John. *Creating and Presenting Hand Puppets.* Florence KY.: Reinhold, 1967.

Bohmer, Gunter. *The Wonderful World of Puppets.* Boston MA.: Plays, 1971.

Boyland, Eleanor. *How To Be a Puppeteer.* New York: McCall Publishing, 1970.

Brody, Vera, and Marie-Francoise Heron. *Fun with Puppets.* New York: Franklin Watts, 1975.

Burano, Remo. *Book of Puppetry* (Edited by Arthur Richmond). New York: Macmillan, 1950.

Bursill, Henry. *Hand Shadows.* New York: Dover, 1967.

————. *More Hand Shadows.* New York: Dover, 1971.

Chernoff, Goldie. *Puppet Party.* New York: Scholastic Book Services, 1971.

Cochrane, Louise. *Shadow Puppets in Color.* Boston MA.: Plays, 1975.

Creegan, George. *Sir George's Book of Hand Puppetry.* Chicago IL.: Follett, 1966.

Cummings, Richard. *101 Hand Puppets.* New York: McKay, 1962.

Currell, David. *The Complete Book of Puppetry.* Boston MA.: Plays, 1975.

Curry, Louis H., and Chester M. Wetzel. *Teaching with Puppets*. Philadelphia PA.: Fortress, 1966.

Engler, Larry, and Carol Fijan. *Making Puppets Come Alive: A Method of Learning and Teaching Hand Puppetry*. New York: Taplinger, 1973.

Fraser, Peter. *Introducing Puppetry*. New York: Watson-Guptill, 1968.

Galdston, Olive. *Play With Puppets*. New York: Play Schools Association, Inc.

Gates, Frieda. *Easy to Make Puppets*. New York: Harvey House Publishers, 1976.

Green, M. C., and B. R. H. Targett. *Space Age Puppets and Masks*. London: George G. Harrap and Co., Ltd., 1969.

Hopper, Grizella H. *Puppet Making Through the Grades*. Worcester MA.: Davis Publications, 1966.

Howard, Vernon. *Puppet and Pantomime Plays*. New York: Sterling Publishing, 1962.

Hutchings, Margaret. *Making and Using Finger Puppets*. New York: Taplinger, 1973.

Jackson, Sheila. *Simple Puppetry*. New York: Watson-Guptil, 1969.

Kampmann, Lothor. *The World of Puppets*. London, England: Evans Brothers Limited, 1972.

Kettelkamp, Larry. *Shadows*. New York: Morrow, 1957.

Leeper, Vera. *Indian Legends Live in Puppetry*. Happy Camp CA.: Naturegraph Publishers, 1973.

Lewis, Shari. *Folding Paper Puppets*. New York: Stein & Day, 1962.

————. *Making Easy Puppets*. New York: Dutton, 1967.

London, Carolyn. *You Can Be a Puppeteer*. Chicago IL.: Moody, 1972.

Luckin, Joyce. *Easy to Make Puppets*. Boston MA.: Plays, 1975.

McNamara, Desmond. *Puppetry*. New York: Horizon Press, 1966.

Morton, Brenda. *Needlework Puppets*. Salem NH.: Faber & Faber, 1964.

Myers, Galene J. *Puppets Can Teach Too*. Minneapolis MN.: Augsburg, 1966.

Ohlson, Kay B. *Felt Puppets*. Harold Mangelson & Sons, 1973.

Paludon, Lis. *Playing with Puppets*. London: Mills and Boon, 1974.

Philpott, A. R. *Let's Look at Puppets*. Chicago IL.: Albert Whitman and Co., 1966.

————. *Modern Puppetry*. Boston MA.: Plays, 1967.

————. *Dictionary of Puppetry*. Boston MA.: Plays, 1969.

Reid, Avis. *Aha! I'm a Puppet*. A. Reid & Associates, 1972.

Reiniger, Lotte. *Shadow Puppets, Shadow Theatres and Shadow Films*. Boston MA.: Plays, 1975.

Renfro, Nancy. *Puppets for Play Production*. New York: Funk & Wagnalls, 1969.

Richter, Dorothy. *Fell's Guide to Hand Puppets: How to Make and Use Them*. New York: Frederick Fell, 1970.

Robinson, Stuart, and Patricia Robinson. *Exploring Puppetry*. New York: Taplinger, 1967.

Ross, Laura. *Hand Puppets: How to Make and Use Them*. New York: Lothrop, Lee & Shepard, 1969.

————. *Puppet Shows, Using Poems and Stories*. New York: Lothrop, Lee & Shepard, 1970.

————. *Finger Puppets: Easy to Make, Fun to Use.* New York: Lothrop, Lee & Shepard, 1971.

Rutter, Vicki. *ABC Puppetry.* Boston MA.: Plays, 1969.

Schonewolf, Herta. *Play with Light and Shadow.* Florence KY: Reinhold, 1968.

Scott, Louis Binder. *Puppets for All Grades.* Owen Publishing, 1966.

Tichenor, Tom. *Folk Plays for Puppets You Can Make.* Nashville, Tenn.: Abingdon Press, 1959.

————. *Tom Tichenor's Puppets.* Nashville, Tenn.: Abingdon Press. 1979.

Union Internationales des Marionettes. *The Puppet Theatre of the Modern World: An International Presentation in Word and Picture.* Boston MA.: Plays, 1967.

Vandergun, Alison. *Puppets for the Classroom.* Lampoon Puppettheatre, 1974.

Wall, Leonard V., et al. *The Puppet Book: A Practical Guide to Puppetry in Schools, Training Colleges and Clubs.* Boston MA.: Plays, 1965.

Wiesner, William. *Hansel and Gretel: A Shadow Puppet Book.* New York: Seabury, 1971.

Worrell, Estell Ansley. *Be a Puppeteer!* New York: McGraw, 1969.

Yerian, Cameron and Margaret Yerian. *Fun Time Puppets and Shadow Plays.* Chicago IL.: Children's Press, 1974.

Puppetry Articles

Alkema, Chester Jay. "The Art of Making Puppets," *Design,* September–October 1966.

Carlson, Ruth Kearney. ''Raising Self-Concepts of Disadvantaged Children Through Puppetry,'' *Elementary English,* March 1970.

Child Craft (Vol. 11), *Make and Do* (1974), pp. 194–203.

Divone, Eileen. ''Puppets, An Educational Experience,'' *School Arts,* September 1977.

Hale, Lucy. ''Simple Puppets in Language Arts,'' *Bits and Pieces,* Bulletin 20-A of the Association for Childhood Education International, 1967.

House and Garden, (October 1966) ''Finger Puppets.''

Hunter, Lynn S. ''Piscataway's Puppet Program,'' *School Library Journal,* May 1977.

Jones, Mrs. Denton and Mrs. Francis Johns. ''Puppet World,'' *School Arts,* June 1970.

Martin, Sister Katherine. ''Classroom Puppetry—from Cereal Boxes to Underwater Environments to . . . Self,'' *Design,* January–February 1978.

Neff, George. ''Let's Have a Tiger for Dinner,'' *School Arts,* November 1970.

Paston, Herbert S. ''Puppets Are Personalities,'' *School Arts,* November 1970.

Quill, Jeane W. ''Puppetry,'' Leaflet 7 in *Creating with Materials for Work and Play.* Association for Childhood Education International, 1969.

Rainey, Sarita. ''Disguising the Paper Bag for Puppetry,'' *School Arts,* November 1967.

Randall, Helen C. ''Puppets Are Fun,'' *School Arts,* June 1977.

Spector, Sima. ''Teaching with No Strings,'' *Grade Teacher,* November 1968.

Sunset (September, 1967), ''Children Can Make Their Own.''

Sylvester, Roland. "Shadow Puppetry in a Design Class," *School Arts*, June 1970.

Vittner, Donald. "Structured Puppet Play Therapy," *Elementary School Guidance and Counseling*, October 1969.

Willis, Margo, and Nancy Quisenberr. "First-Grade Puffitry," *Early Years*, January 1976.

Yoder, R. A. "Puppets," *School Arts*, June 1970.

The Puppeteers of America, Inc., publish *The Puppetry Journal* six times a year. Order from:
    Mrs. Gayle Schluter
    #5 Cricklewood Path
    Pasadena, CA 91107

An annotated list of puppetry books is available from:
    The Puppetry Store
    Jennifer Ukstins, Director
    14316 Sturtevant Road
    Silver Spring, MD 20904

Other References

Austin, Lou. *The Little Me and The Great Me*. Capon Springs, W.Va.: Partnership Foundation, 1957.

————. *My Secret Power: A New, More Meaningful Version of The Cinderella Story*. Capon Springs, W.VA.: Partnership Foundation, 1961.

Barksdale, L. S. *Building Self-Esteem*. Idyllwild, CA.: The Barksdale Foundation, 1972.

————. *Essays on Self-Esteem*. Idyllwild CA: The Barksdale Foundation, 1972.

Briggs, Dorothy Corkillo. *Your Child's Self-Esteem: The Key To His Life*. Garden City, N.Y.: Doubleday, 1967.

Ginott, Haim G. *Teacher and Child: A Book for Parents and Teachers*. New York: Macmillan, 1972.